SOUTH

OF **49**

SOUTH OF 49

THE CANADIAN GUIDE TO BUYING RESIDENTIAL REAL ESTATE IN THE UNITED STATES

PHILIP McKERNAN

DAN SAMPSON | MIKE CUNNING

John Wiley & Sons Canada, Ltd.

Library and Archives Canada Cataloguing in Publication Data

McKernan, Philip
   South of 49 : the Canadian guide to buying residential real estate in the United States / Philip McKernan, Dan Sampson, Mike Cunning.

Includes index.
ISBN 978-0-470-16131-9

   1. Residential real estate—Purchasing—United States. 2. Residential real estate—United States. 3. Real estate investment—United States. I. Sampson, Dan II. Cunning, Mike III. Title.

HD259.M388 2009   332.63'240973   C2009-905122-2

Production Credits
Cover design: Adrian So
Interior design: Pat Loi
Typesetter: Thomson Digital
Printer: Friesens
Cover image: Mint Girl Productions/Photodisc/Getty

John Wiley & Sons Canada, Ltd.
6045 Freemont Blvd.
Mississauga, Ontario
L5R 4J3

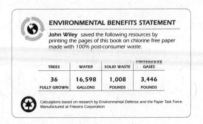

ENVIRONMENTAL BENEFITS STATEMENT

John Wiley saved the following resources by printing the pages of this book on chlorine free paper made with 100% post-consumer waste.

TREES	WATER	SOLID WASTE	GREENHOUSE GASES
36	16,598	1,008	3,446
FULLY GROWN	GALLONS	POUNDS	POUNDS

Calculations based on research by Environmental Defense and the Paper Task Force. Manufactured at Friesens Corporation

Printed in Canada
1 2 3 4 5 FP 13 12 11 10 09

Table of Contents

Acknowledgments   vii

Introduction   1

Chapter 1:   Of Risk and Reward   5

Chapter 2:   Of Phoenix and Foreclosures   11

Chapter 3:   Of a Team and a Dream   29

Chapter 4:   Of Florida and Mount Everest   43

Chapter 5:   Of Experts and Equity   71

Chapter 6:   Of Ownership, Death and Taxes   93

Chapter 7:   Of a California Lifestyle and a Nevada Auction   121

Chapter 8:   Of Phoenix and Palm Springs, and
             Narrowing the Search   161

Chapter 9:   Of Offers and Counter-Offers   193

Chapter 10: Of Escrow Officers and Closing the Deal   217

Chapter 11: Victory   235

Epilogue   243

Index   249

Acknowledgments

Writing a book was an enormous task and one that I have to say I completely underestimated. I also didn't fully appreciate, until the project was launched, the power of having the right people around to help shape the material and share the experience. Looking back, I must say this daunting task would not have been possible without some key people.

In the middle of writing the book, my wife Pauline and I had our first child, Charlie. As is the case with any newborn, they simply (or not so simply) arrive into your life and don't care about book deadlines, business, or if you get to the gym on any given day. While I did consider putting Charlie on eBay some nights (just kidding, Charlie!), his presence changed my life forever, and for the better.

While my wife was in labour, I was asked to do a television interview related to this book. While my son may never forgive me, Pauline insisted I keep the commitment. This is typical of Pauline, who has been a huge believer in me since we met. Her support for everything I do inspires me to take on projects outside my comfort zone. Pauline, you are my hero.

Speaking of mothers, I have to mention mine. I am a big believer in "we are who we meet," and I can't help but think that many of the good traits I have come from her. The mentoring my father gave me has crafted my ability to attract great people into my life, which has led to this book being possible.

Mentors have played a huge part in my life, and here are just some of the amazing people I have met along an incredible journey so far: Trevor Garret, Anthony Clare, Les Hewitt, Keith Cunningham, Michael Vaughan, Shane Cradock, Robert McKernan, David McKernan, Stephen O'Reilly, and Don Campbell. Your belief has been my oxygen, and my hope is to make you all proud.

To my numerous clients and groups that I have had the pleasure to mentor: You are my fuel and you push me every day to be better than I was the day before.

In December 2007, I met Don Loney of John Wiley & Sons Canada, who, although I did not realize it at the time, was to have a huge impact on my life. He introduced himself after hearing me deliver a keynote speech at a real estate conference in Toronto, and he later suggested I consider writing a book. Since then, he has supported and trusted me personally, as well as my *South of 49* team. Thank you Don, for your belief in us.

A huge thanks also go out to my co-authors, Dan Sampson and Mike Cunning, who graciously accepted my invitation to participate in this project. They brought a fountain of knowledge to the book, some adventure, and a lot of laughs on the many trips we took to the U.S. while doing research.

Last but certainly not least, on behalf of the authors I would like to thank Brenda Bouw who helped us craft this book from an idea into what it is today. I'm not entirely sure if writing or patience is Brenda's greatest gift, but I know for certain we tested the latter. Your genuine interest, determination, honest feedback, and military-type deadlines were not just appreciated but a critical part of the project. I could not have imagined doing this project without you.

Philip McKernan
May 2009

Introduction

Buying a home in the United States is a goal for many Canadians. Sitting by the pool or playing a round of golf in January while your neighbors back home are shoveling snow is, for many, the Canadian dream.

Statistics show that more and more Canadians are making that dream a reality. By mid-2008, nearly one quarter of all international homebuyers in the US were Canadians. This was not only a record, but also more than double the year before. According to the 2008 National Association of Realtors annual profile of international home buying activity in the US, the sun states of Florida and Arizona, not surprisingly, were the most popular locations for Canadian buyers, accounting for more than 60 per cent of their purchases. The survey also showed many Canadians paid cash for those homes.

House prices in the US are the cheapest they've been for some time, which is one of many factors inspiring Canadians to buy property there. Some are looking for a retirement home, while others are scouring the market for investment opportunities. The subprime mortgage mess has reduced prices by about 25 per cent in the US since the peak in 2006, and by more than 40 per cent in some states, in particular those sun destinations of Florida and Arizona which were overbuilt.

Foreclosures are so common in the US that, in true competitive American style, cities boast their top spots on the foreclosure capital standings.

While buying a sunbelt home is not new to Canadians—even before the housing market meltdown—more are inspired to buy when the Canadian dollar nears parity with the US dollar. And as home prices in Canada were reaching their peak, many homeowners took equity out of their Canadian properties to put towards buying a US place. Even after the Canadian economy and housing market began to feel their own pressures, the land rush south of the border continued, thanks to low property values and high foreclosure rates.

In fact, as long as there is winter in Canada, Canadians will continue to take the US property plunge. The purchases will also continue to be driven by demographics in the foreseeable future. As the Baby Boom generation ages, more and more are looking for retirement properties in vacation destinations for their families during the cold winter months. But instead of just renting a place, or going for long hotel stays, many are looking to buy something of their own.

The American housing crisis has also become an investment opportunity for Canadians not yet ready for retirement. The strategy: buy a home or condo to generate cash flow, and eventually sell it down the road when the market recovers.

Whether it's a lifestyle purchase or an investment, there are many factors about buying US property that many Canadian buyers understandably find confusing, or they overlook. Add to that the complexities of the new foreclosure-driven buyers' market, and buying a US property could be a recipe for disaster if you don't do your homework.

That's where *South of 49* comes in. This book is about more than just tax advice and buying tips. We take you through all of the real-life considerations when buying down south, from travel time and immigration rules to making sure the home or condo you buy actually fits your investment goals. We will also help you answer one very important question when considering such a purchase: Why? Why should you buy a place and not just rent? Why should you buy in Florida instead of California, for example? The answers? It all depends. It depends on you, your individual circumstances and your goals. This book will help you think through these decisions before you make them.

While owning a home in the US may be the Canadian dream, it's also not for everyone. We aren't trying to discourage you from buying. Instead, we want to help you make the right choice. Buying a house in the US is a huge commitment. It's also a lot of work. Our goal is to get you to do your research first, and then consider carefully whether the investment is right for you.

Sound daunting? Don't worry; it will also be a lot of fun. That's because we plan to share this information through two very entertaining characters: Ted, the Textbook Emotionally Driven buyer, and his friend Sid, the Sophisticated Investor Dude. Ted and Sid, old university buddies with different goals, will show you, as a Canadian, the pros and cons of buying and owning your own piece of property in the US.

While Ted and Sid are fictional characters, most of their experiences are based on actual events. We, the authors, have a great deal of experience in buying and selling real estate in our professional lives. For this book in particular, we traveled to several US cities from coast to coast and visited dozens of homes for sale as part of our research. We also had long discussions with various players in the American housing market, from buyers and sellers to realtors, developers, inspectors and everyone in between. We had a lot of fun, and we learned a ton. It's our pleasure to share our insights, experiences and overall adventure with you.

Philip McKernan
Dan Sampson
Mike Cunning
North Vancouver, May 2009

1
Of Risk and Reward

We meet Ted and Sid, and Ted's real estate venture begins. Ted looked up from the Risk board game laid out on the table before him and directly into the eyes of his old friend, Sid. Ted knew what was next, as Sid flashed him that trademark winning smile that Ted has learned to recognize since they shared a university dorm room nearly 20 years earlier.

Sid threw up his arms in victory.

"Yes! The United States of America is mine!" Sid shouted after having moved his red armies into Ted's last remaining stronghold.

Sid then jumped up and began a victory dance across Ted's living room.

"That, Ted my friend, is what world domination looks like," Sid said as he continued his winning gyrations.

Ted tried his best to look disconsolate. Then he laughed. "Congratulations buddy," he said, accepting defeat in the latest round of the game that had become a tradition whenever the two got together.

"You won this time. But I, my friend, will own my own part of the US soon enough," Ted said. "For real. And if you don't stop that prancing around, I won't ever invite you over."

Sid stopped and looked at Ted, puzzled.

"All of this ocean air in Vancouver is making you talk funny," Sid said. "Maybe you should come back to Toronto with me and start thinking straight again."

Ted shook his head and smiled.

"Seriously, Sid. I'm about to own my own sweet little property in Phoenix, and when those Toronto winters get you down, maybe you can come visit—especially during hurricane season when you can't see through your boarded-up windows at your Florida place."

Sid sat down.

"Are you serious? When were you and Nancy in Phoenix? What property? Did her parents buy a place down there?"

"No," said Ted. "We are buying a place, or maybe I should I say I am. Nancy isn't too keen on putting any of her own money in it just yet, but I've got some inheritance money from years ago and maybe she'll agree to invest in the place too once she sees it. I mean, it sounds great and . . ."

"Whoa!" Sid interrupted. "Hold on a minute Ted. What do you mean it *sounds* great? You haven't seen it?"

"I don't need to see it. I have the listing right here. And besides, there are tons of photos on the Internet, and a virtual tour," Ted said as he pulled a sheet of paper out from a stack of magazines on the coffee table beside him. "I found it on the Internet and it sounds perfect. It's so cheap; it's practically a steal. The last owners bought it for $325,000 in 2006 and now it's for sale for $185,000. It's barely lived in—what could be wrong with it? Maybe I'll have to finish the basement or something. At that price, I still win. I can't even buy a garage in Vancouver that cheap!"

Sid grabbed the listing from Ted's hands and started to read the description out loud: "Very nice home built in 2005. Bank owned. Priced to Sell! Barely lived in. Three thousand square feet. This home features three bedrooms, two-and-a-half bathrooms, eat-in kitchen and dining room, living room. Close to park and rec centre. Needs a little elbow grease . . ."

Sid read the rest quietly under his breath.

"Ted, friend. I don't know about this. 'Needs a little elbow grease?' Who gave this to you?"

"A realtor in Phoenix," Ted said. "I saw an ad from him in the local paper. He sets it all up for you from down there. He sounds like a really good guy. You tell him what you want, you know, a pool or not, a garage, how close you want to be to the center of town or the golf club. He said this one is pretty close to the US Airways Centre where the Phoenix Suns play, which is right near Chase Field, where the Diamondbacks play baseball. And the price, Sid, *it's soooo cheap*. Almost half what the owners paid for it! I can't believe how much house prices have dropped down there. It's the perfect time for me to buy!"

"Stop right there, Ted," Sid said.

Ted noticed his friend's smug smile had suddenly turned to a look of concern. He'd seen this face from Sid before—the last time was when he bought a boat on impulse. Sid recommended he try renting a boat a few times first, to gauge how often he would actually use it. Ted bought the boat anyway, and after the excitement of being captain of his own ship wore off, the boat seldom left the marina while the docking and service fees ate away at his wallet. He sold the boat after two summers for less than he paid for it. Sid's concern scared him.

"Oh no," Ted said sheepishly. "What have I done this time?"

"Not to worry my friend," Sid said, his tone *almost* reassuring. "But, you haven't put any money down on this yet have you? Please tell me you haven't put any money down yet, Ted?"

"I have tied it up with a deposit—a thousand bucks—and conditions are removed on Tuesday," Ted said defensively.

Sid leaned forward and looked directly at his friend, who had since sunk into his chair.

"Listen, just do me one little favor, would you?" Sid asked.

Ted sighed, but kept listening.

"Just go down and see the place for yourself first," Sid advised. "Go this weekend. Take a couple days off and make it a long weekend if you can. If you love it, if it's really the place you've always dreamed of having as a vacation home, or investment, or whatever, then do it. But don't—and Ted I'm begging you here, as your friend—don't buy it without seeing it first. Please?"

Ted rubbed his eyes with the palms of his hands then shook his head, as if he had just been splashed with a bucket of cold water.

"All right Sid, if you insist. I'll go see it. But it's expensive to fly down there. And I have to get the time off work first, and . . ."

Sid interrupted again.

"Ted, it's not a set of golf clubs you're buying here. It's a house. If you're complaining about the price . . . By the way, what is the plan? Are you planning to rent this out or . . ."

"I know, I know, Sid. You're right," Ted cut in. "You are always right. Okay, I'll get down there and meet this realtor myself. But I'm telling you right now that this place is the one. You'll see. As for my plan, I don't know exactly. Maybe I'll rent it out to friends. It would be nice to live there someday too. All I know is that if I don't buy now, I'll be kicking myself later."

Sid wasn't so sure Ted understood what he was getting into, but felt he had pushed his old friend enough for one night. Sid took another tack.

"I hope you are right, Ted," Sid said. "I can't wait for you to tell me 'I told you so.' And if you want, call me when you're down there, let me know how it looks or if you have any questions or anything."

"Yes, 'Dad,' " Ted said, laughing. "Now, can we change the subject?"

He then glared at Sid, like an eagle stalking its prey.

"How about another round of Risk then, eh pal? This time I'll show you who owns the US. Get your little army ready for General Ted!"

The two laughed as they set up the game. "You're always full of surprises," Sid said. "That's what makes you Ted, I guess. Hey, remember that boat you bought a few years ago and never used?"

"Just roll the damn dice," Ted said.

SID'S TIPS

- Never buy a property in the US, or anywhere for that matter, without seeing it in person first. Internet photos and realtors' brochures aren't remotely enough information on which to base a purchasing decision. You need to see the property for yourself, including talking to the neighbors and taking a tour of the neighborhood and the region. You need to compare your list of desired services and amenities against those available where you're looking.

- Don't put down a deposit unless you are clear about the terms and conditions, including asking whether you can get your money back if you change your mind and don't buy.

- Remember that listings are trying to sell you features of the home. They're marketing tools. Any mention of "needs elbow grease" or "handyman's special" is a red flag that the house needs a thorough inspection that may require more than just hiring a home inspector.

- Just because a house has fallen dramatically in price doesn't make it a good reason to buy. It could be the opposite. What looks like a "good deal" should never be the primary motivating factor in a purchasing decision.

- Have a plan. What do you intend to do with the property? Will you be the only occupant or do you plan to rent it out? Think about this before you even start looking at buying a property in the US.

2

Of Phoenix and Foreclosures

Ted awoke to the harsh "Beep! Beep! Beep!" of his alarm clock. He felt the sharp poke of an elbow from his wife Nancy in his right rib. She then rolled over and held a pillow over her head to muffle the sound. Ted rolled in the opposite direction and silenced the alarm with the slap of his hand. He opened his eyes. In bright red numbers, the clock read 4:01 a.m. Suddenly, Ted remembered why he set it so early. He had a plane to catch. This was the day he was to fly to Phoenix to buy his dream home.

As he pushed himself upright, Ted thought to himself, "I bet Donald Trump never has to get up this early." He shuffled to the en suite to grab a shower, walking past his already packed suitcase, his backpack with his passport zippered into a side pocket, the *Lonely Planet* guide to Phoenix and, of course, the listing of what would soon be his new home away from home.

The cab arrived on schedule at 5 a.m. Ted ignored the impulse to shout goodbye to Nancy as he headed out the door. As he stepped out into the pouring rain, he reflected that he wouldn't get up if he didn't have to, especially on a soggy Saturday in November.

The driver tucked Ted's luggage in the trunk of the cab and hopped into the driver's seat. The driver picked up his

Starbucks coffee in a Venti cup, said good morning and asked, "Where are you flying to?"

"Phoenix," Ted replied. "International departures, please. I'm going to Phoenix. My flight's at seven."

The driver nodded and started the 30-minute drive to the airport. Ted settled back and watched the rain slide across the car window. Traffic built as they approached the airport, and Ted thought how surprising it was to see so many people up at this hour. "How many might own property down south?" he mused.

At the airport, Ted checked in with his airline and made his way to the customs and immigration area, which he had to pass through before going to his departure gate. When he turned the corner, he saw about 50 people already in the lineup ahead of him. He yawned and did the step, stop and stand dance along with his fellow travelers for about 30 minutes. Finally, it was his turn. Ted flipped open his passport with his thumb and handed his ticket to the stone-faced immigration officer.

"Where to?" the woman behind the counter said in a curt voice.

"Phoenix."

She then asked a series of questions including: What was the purpose of his visit? How long was he staying? Where was he staying? What was the address? Ted knew everything but the address. He told her it was a Holiday Inn Express.

"I'm sure I'll be well rested, if the hotel is really as good as those ads say. I like those ads, don't you?" Ted asked.

The officer looked up at Ted, expressionless, and handed him back his passport and ticket.

"Next!" she shouted to the person behind him.

Ted felt as though he had just run into his old high school football coach. He, too, was a tough nut with absolutely no sense of humor! Ted shrugged it off and began his search for caffeine. After a few sips of coffee, Ted spotted some empty seats outside his departure gate. Using his backpack as a pillow, he stretched out across three seats and fell asleep. It seemed as though he had just closed his eyes when a tap on his shoulder woke him.

"Are you flying to Phoenix with us today, sir?" asked a flight attendant with a brunette bob haircut, looking down at him.

Ted nodded, jumped up, grabbed his backpack, and followed her through the gate and on to the plane.

As he headed down the aisle and into the plane towards his seat near the back, Ted observed the usual pre-takeoff rituals: passengers cramming luggage into overhead bins, fidgeting with headsets, adjusting their seatbelts and complaining to the crew. People were being packed in pretty tightly, he thought. He decided to focus instead on one happy-looking couple sitting silently, dressed like twins in bright floral shirts, shorts, sandals with socks and dark tans. Ted smiled and reflected: "That will be me and Nancy someday soon." After settling into his middle seat, Ted blew up his air-filled neck pillow and prepared for the first of two flights taking him to Phoenix today.

WELCOME TO PHOENIX

"Ladies and gentleman, we'll be landing shortly in Phoenix. Please ensure your tray tables are put away and your seats are fully upright."

The flight attendant's voice was like music to Ted's ears. After nearly six hours in the air, not including a 90-minute stopover, he had finally arrived. Ted calculated how long the trip had taken so far. He got up at 4:00 in the morning Vancouver time, and finally arrived in Phoenix at around 2:00 in the afternoon, Phoenix time. He set his watch. As the plane made its descent, he calculated how much money the trip had cost him so far: flight, about $700; cab, $50; hotel, $220. He figured he could get a cheaper flight by booking earlier, but he didn't have time to really prepare for the trip. Sid had insisted he go right away. No matter—the money was spent. Besides, Ted was sure everything was cheaper in the US. And, the Phoenix realtor said the house was only a 20-minute drive from the airport. Soon he'd see his new place.

As the plane circled above Phoenix's Sky Harbor International Airport, Ted got his first taste of this big city. As he surveyed the urban sprawl, Ted wondered where he would even begin looking for a place if he didn't already have one picked out. What a coincidence it was that he found that realtor's ad in the paper, he thought. It must be fate.

After landing and collecting his luggage, Ted walked out of the airport toward the shuttle to the car rental depot. As he stepped outside, he suddenly felt the desert heat wrap around him like a blanket. Ted smiled, pointed his face toward the sun, put on his sunglasses and exhaled loudly. "This is my kind of weather," he said, and then stepped on the bus.

After what seemed like another long journey, Ted finally arrived at the rental car building and was given the keys to his vehicle, a beige sedan. He tossed his luggage in the back seat and headed out of the parking lot with a map of Phoenix laid open on his lap and a printout of the directions that Cliff, the realtor, had emailed him. Ted had to meet Cliff at 3 p.m. at the house. It was now 2:30. He started the drive.

At 2:55, the announcer on the radio said the temperature had hit the day's high of 95 degrees Fahrenheit. Ted did the math quickly in his head. "Wow, 35 degrees Celsius in November!" he said out loud to himself in the car. It almost never gets that hot in Vancouver.

Ted pulled off the freeway at the appropriate exit and passed rows of strip malls and drive-in fast-food outlets. "I'll never get hungry in this neighborhood," he said, talking to himself again. He continued to follow the realtor's directions, on the lookout for Jefferson Lane, a right-hand turn Ted expected to approach soon. He drove for blocks. Ten minutes passed and he still hadn't hit Jefferson. What's worse, every street looked the same and he couldn't tell if he was lost, or just not there yet. What struck Ted more, though, as he drove was the number of houses with "For Sale" or "Bank Owned" signs out front. There must have been a half dozen of them on every block. Ted had heard a lot about this subprime mess in the US, but now saw it for himself. As he drove along, Ted realized he hadn't seen a lot of people around this area, or many cars either. Maybe it was just too hot to be outside at this time of day. Maybe people were hanging out in their backyard pools. He kept driving. Finally, Ted pulled over and once again consulted the map. Many of the streets he crossed weren't listed on it.

"Must be an old map," Ted said to himself. He looked up and spotted a 7-Eleven sign a block ahead. He pulled up, stepped inside to a blast of air-conditioning and grabbed a Gatorade from the fridge. He then walked over to the cash register to pay, but first asked the clerk for directions to Jefferson Lane.

"Never heard of it," said the pudgy teenage boy behind the counter. "But I'm not from around here. Not many people live in this part of town."

Ted sighed. He decided to just pay for the drink and call Cliff the realtor for directions. As he opened his wallet, Ted realized he forgot to get American money before he left. He planned the trip in such a hurry that he forgot about the change in currency.

"I don't suppose you take Canadian money?" Ted asked the clerk, who was sucking back a Big Gulp.

"No sir, just American money here. But there's a bank back up on the highway there."

"Never mind," Ted said. He grabbed a bag of Doritos from the shelf beside him and a sealed-up turkey sandwich from the cooler and paid with his Visa card. Ted then called Cliff for directions to the house. Cliff said he was about five minutes away. It was 3:30 p.m. Ted apologized for being late and promised to be right over.

Fifteen minutes later, Ted rolled into the driveway of "his" new home, behind the realtor's BMW, which he noticed had a couple dents on the driver's side. Ted stepped out of the car towards Cliff, who was standing outside the front door of the house.

"Whew, it sure is hot here, eh?" Ted said.

As Cliff started to speak, there was a loud roar from above. Ted ducked, by instinct.

"Wow, what was that!?"

"Oh, that's just a fighter jet," said Cliff, who was wearing a beige button-down short-sleeve shirt and wrap-around shades. Beads of sweat rolled down his forehead.

"There's a military base not too far from here. Makes you feel safe, doesn't it?"

Ted, dressed in a Vancouver Canucks T-shirt and jeans, looked up at the sky and said: "I guess that's pretty cool."

Cliff nodded then gestured for Ted to follow him into the house. Ted noticed the front lawn had a number of new shrubs and trees poking out of a patch of brown grass.

He then slowly scanned the outside of the house, making note of the yellow stucco exterior, the clay tile roof, bay windows and double-car garage.

"It sure is big, isn't it?" Ted said.

"It's a beauty," Cliff replied. "A great neighborhood. Wait until you see inside."

INSIDE JEFFERSON LANE

As the front door of the home swung open, Ted noticed a faded sign in red ink that read: "Foreclosure. Bank Owned." Cliff was watching and before Ted could comment said: "It's a shame, isn't it? There are a lot of them around here. But it's a steal for a guy like you. I mean, nearly half price from what the guy before you bought it for."

"I know," Ted said, his voice rose with excitement. "My house back home has gone up in value almost as much as this one's gone down. It's amazing isn't it? And it doesn't even rain here eight months of the year!"

As they walked through the front hall, Ted's first thought was how big the place was—and how empty. It also smelled like new paint and new carpet.

"The carpet is brand new," Cliff said.

Ted noticed there were no covers on the light switches and pointed it out to Cliff, who then pointed to a stack of switch plates on the kitchen counter.

"They'll be put up today. We didn't expect you so soon, Ted, so you might see a few unfinished things," Cliff said.

Ted followed Cliff through the main floor of the house and listened to him talk about the square footage, the type of windows installed and on which side of the house the sun rose and set.

The next stage of tour was the second floor. As they approached the stairwell, Cliff stopped and turned to Ted. His voice got deeper.

"Now, remember I told you the place needed a bit of sweat equity. You'll see what I mean up here. Don't be concerned. It's an easy fix. I know a guy who can do it for you for less than most."

As they climbed the stairs, Ted noticed the drywall was rippled, like freshly raked sand. Ted felt a pull in his stomach. The walls looked even worse at the top of the stairs. He then looked down the hallway and saw a huge hole in the wall. It looked like someone had smashed it with a wrecking ball.

"They have a lot of parties here, the last owners?" Ted said with a nervous laugh.

"It's a hell of a story," Cliff replied.

He then proceeded to tell Ted about the previous owner, who was forced out of the home by the bank. But the owner didn't want to leave. In fact, he decided one day, in a 120-degree heat wave, to barricade himself in the home. Police were called. They tried to persuade the man to leave, but he refused. After about an hour, the sheriff decided to take matters into his own hands. He went to the trunk of his car and took out what looked like a piece of silly putty. He slapped it on the outside wall of the room the man had holed himself in.

"A few seconds later, Boom! And there's your proof," Cliff said, pointing to the hole. "The guy didn't stand a chance. Not sure what happened to him after that. I mean, he's okay, but I don't know what kind of trouble he is in. Poor bastard."

Ted stood with his mouth wide open. He was speechless.

"Yup," Cliff continued. "Ever heard of Composition C-4? It's a common variety of military plastic explosive. Wouldn't be surprised if he got it right off the base over there."

Ted walked closer to the wall, and was about to touch the surface when Cliff stopped him.

"Oh, I wouldn't touch that if I were you. How soon are you headed back to Canada? Tomorrow? Monday? Don't want that on your skin when you are passing through immigration. They might think you're a terrorist."

Ted pulled his hand back. He decided it was a good time to call Sid. He knew what Sid would say. Ted had a bad feeling, but he tried to stay positive. Maybe he could fix that wall? How much could it cost? Plus, he had done a little dry walling in the past. How hard could it be?

Ted excused himself, went out to the front lawn and called Sid in Toronto.

"I've been waiting for your call," Sid said. "How's the house? What do you think?"

Ted described the house, how big it was, and then told him about the hole in the wall and how it happened.

"Ted, that's not good," Sid said in his concerned voice.

"First, you can't fix that yourself. You would have to hire someone. As a visitor, you don't want to be seen as working illegally in the US. They have rules about that sort of thing. Also, how do you know for sure that the former owner isn't going to come back again and try to break in? He may not be over it yet, even after the explosion. Geez, Ted, a little elbow grease?"

As Ted tried to convince Sid it might not be as bad as it sounds, more jets flew overhead.

"What was that?" Sid asked.

"The fighter jets," Ted said. "You could hear that?"

"Hear it? Ted, is your house on the tarmac?"

Ted paced the sidewalk in front of the house and listened to Sid trying to talk him out of the purchase.

"Maybe get him to show you something else," Sid said.

Ted felt like a fool. He walked back into the house and heard Cliff saying goodbye to someone on his cell phone.

"I think I made a mistake," Ted said. "I can't do this. You didn't tell me it was this bad. Don't you have something else I can see? I mean, I gave you a thousand bucks and I came all the way down here?"

Cliff didn't seem surprised by Ted's reaction.

"Listen, I've got another house down the street you could see. Never lived in. It actually costs about $10,000 less. Want to see it?"

"Does it need more work than this one?" Ted asked.

The realtor explained to him that, in fact, the other house didn't need any work. The prices in the market were sporadic, which had less to do with the condition of the homes and more to do with what the bank stuck with the property wanted to sell it for.

"Give me a minute," Ted said, running out into the middle of the deserted street.

"Stupid! Stupid! Stupid!" Ted muttered to himself, as he banged his hand against his forehead.

Cliff was watching through the front window. He waited a few minutes then stepped out to talk to Ted.

"Let me show you this place two doors over," he said.

Ted followed, but didn't speak.

The house looked the same as his C4 "dream home," and also had a "Bank Owned" sign on it.

"Ted, come inside. I think you'll really like this one. No elbow grease. And it's never been lived in," Cliff said.

Ted took the tour, but didn't hear a word Cliff said. All he could think about was how he almost bought the first house without even seeing it first, and how right Sid was in forcing him to come down and visit. Nancy was also right to be skeptical. He started to doubt whether he was capable of buying real estate in the US, and began to think about how much money he wasted on this latest whim. The impulsive boat purchase suddenly seemed small by comparison.

Ted walked over to Cliff, who was talking about the features in the kitchen. "Thanks, but I'm out," Ted said. "And I don't suppose I can get my deposit back."

"Unfortunately, Ted, no."

"Forget it," Ted said, then walked out of the house and straight for his rental car.

As he put the car in reverse and turned to look behind him, Ted heard a knock on the passenger-side window. It was Cliff.

"You know, I was going to mention this but I think we could get the first house for $165,000 if we put in an offer today."

Ted, still shocked that the realtor never mentioned the gaping hole in the house, yelled back: "No, thanks!" and drove away.

PHOENIX RISES AGAIN

As he drove, Ted heard on the radio that the Phoenix Suns were playing at home that night and tickets were still available. He decided to go to the game. After the day he just had, Ted felt he deserved some fun. He consulted the map for directions to the US Airways Center. It turned out it was nowhere near the home he saw earlier in the day, despite what Cliff said in his listing. Instead of getting upset again, Ted decided then and there to put the whole C4 house experience behind him and enjoy the game and the city, where he was to spend another couple of days. Tonight, he'd watch basketball and tomorrow he would golf.

Ted bought the cheapest ticket he could find and headed to the concession for a beer and hotdog before finding his seat, which was right behind the Suns bench, although high up in the nosebleeds. He sat back and soaked up the atmosphere. He hadn't been to a professional basketball game since the Grizzlies left Vancouver years earlier. About halfway through the first quarter, Ted overheard a conversation behind him between two men. They were talking about buying real estate.

"Where are you guys from?" Ted said as he turned to the men, who looked like brothers, and were about his age.

"Calgary," said the man on Ted's right wearing a Suns jersey. "You?"

"Vancouver. Nice to meet you," Ted said and all three raised their plastic beer cups to toast their Canadian heritage.

"I couldn't help but overhear you guys talking about buying real estate. Are you in the market down here?" Ted asked.

"I just bought a place," the jersey-wearing man said. "It's a condo. I'm planning to rent it out. Got a great deal on it. My agent is a genius!"

Ted was intrigued.

"My brother here is thinking about buying, but he's too chicken," the man continued.

Ted then told them about his day, the house he saw and the agent he now wished he had never met.

"That's some bad luck, my friend," said the man in the jersey, who introduced himself as Al, and his brother Pete. "Hey,

I can give you the number of my agent, Sam. You won't find a better one, in my opinion. A real straight shooter, originally from Texas."

Al wrote the agent's name and telephone number on the back of napkin and handed it to Ted.

"I'm serious, don't forget to call . . . oh, hold on, wait, score!" Al yelled and raised both hands in the air. The Suns scored again. Ted thanked Al for the tip and turned back around to watch the rest of the game.

When the game was over, Ted shook hands with his new friends, and promised to give Al's realtor a call the next time he was in town.

"Great to meet you," said Ted.

Again, to Ted, it felt like fate. Maybe his real estate dream wasn't over after all.

Phoenix

Between 2002 and 2008, Phoenix had grown 24.2 per cent, making it the second-fastest-growing metropolitan area in the United States, following only Las Vegas. Phoenix was one of the hardest hit by the subprime mortgage crisis. In early 2009, the median home price was $150,000, down from its $262,000 peak in recent years.

The City

Phoenix is the state capital of Arizona. Its main districts include: Downtown, Midtown, West Phoenix, North Phoenix, South Phoenix, Biltmore Area, Arcadia, Sunnyslope, Ahwatukee.

The Economy

Many of its residents are employed by the government. It is also home to a handful of large US corporations, including waste management company Allied Waste, electronics firm Avnet, Apollo Group (which operates the University of Phoenix), mining company Freeport-McMoRan (recently merged with Phoenix-based Phelps Dodge), retailer PetSmart, energy supplier Pinnacle West and retailer CSK Auto. Phoenix is also home to the headquarters of moving supply and rental company U-HAUL International and the Best Western hotel chain. Intel also has one of its largest sites in the city.

The Military

The military has a significant presence in Phoenix, with Luke Air Force Base located in the western suburbs. At its height, in the 1940s, the military in the Phoenix area had three bases: Luke Field (still in use), Falcon Field, and Williams Air Force Base (now Phoenix-Mesa Gateway Airport), with numerous auxiliary airfields located in the region.

Sports

Phoenix is home to the Arizona Cardinals National Football League team, the Arizona Diamondbacks of Major League Baseball, the Phoenix Suns in the National Basketball Association and the Phoenix Coyotes of the National Hockey League.

Source: **www.wikipedia.org**.

BACK TO VANCOUVER, EMPTY-HANDED

Shortly after 10 p.m. on Monday, Ted returned to his house in Vancouver after three days in Phoenix. He dropped his bags on the floor and shouted from the front door: "Nancy, I'm home."

Nancy came out from the living room and shuffled toward Ted dressed in her housecoat and fuzzy slippers. She gave him a big hug and kiss on the cheek.

"Poor Ted. There will be other homes," she said.

Nancy was being sweet, but Ted knew she was secretly gloating. She knew something would go wrong. He hadn't yet told her about the new agent whose name he got from his new Calgary friends. Ted decided to wait a bit longer before popping the real estate question to Nancy again.

"Looks like you got some sun down there?" she said.

"Yeah, I played golf yesterday. Had a great time."

"Good for you. I'm glad you had some fun," Nancy said. "I'm off to bed. See you shortly."

She headed to their room upstairs while Ted dragged his luggage into the laundry room in the basement. As he opened his suitcase, Ted noticed the contents were turned upside down. His dirty socks were no longer tucked in the side pockets and his shaving cream was splattered across most of his clothing. "Someone has been through my bag!" He then realized the significance of the bright orange TSA (Transportation Security Administration) sticker on the front of his suitcase. His bag had been searched. He shrugged. Nothing surprised him after the trip he just took.

Ted felt tired, but not quite ready to sleep. He headed to the living room, plopped down on the couch and turned the television on to his favorite sports channel. Ted was watching the hockey highlights when he noticed a pile of mail on the coffee table in front of him. He sifted though it—gas bill, telephone bill, *Sports Illustrated*, *Maclean's* and Saturday's newspaper. Ted tossed the pile on the couch beside him when out from the bottom slipped a glossy flyer with a giant palm tree on the cover. Ted turned to look at the headline which read: "Florida: Land of Good Living. How to own your own piece of the Sunshine State."

"Hmm," he mused, scratching his head as he flipped through the flyer. "I never even considered Florida."

Ted remembered Sid had some property in Florida, rentals and his own vacation home he bought recently. Maybe if he followed Sid's strategy he would have better luck. Maybe he would decide to buy in Florida *and* Phoenix! Ted smiled at how his dream had suddenly grown to two homes—one on each side of the Sunbelt. He laughed to himself.

"First I have to get Nancy to agree to one place," Ted thought, then picked up the TV remote and started channel surfing.

TED'S TIPS

- When booking a flight to the US, especially a sun destination, check for charters or other deals. Book as early as possible.

- Remember to take American money with you. You can also use Canadian bankcards at most US bank machines to withdraw American money.

- Be ready for long lineups at customs and immigration counters. Also be prepared to answer questions about your trip such as: Where you are going? How long are you staying? The purpose of your visit? Where will you be staying? What is the address of where you will be staying? While Ted got lucky and didn't have to provide this information, it can be a requirement.

- Get more information on the realtor who is selling the home. Ask more questions about the home and its condition *before* you travel. Don't be afraid to ask as many questions as possible.

- Find out how much other homes in the area are selling for and how they compare to the one you're interested in. Essential comparables: square footage; number of bedrooms and bathrooms; upgrades; pool; landscaping; garage; overall condition.

- Be careful when renovating your own US property if you're not a citizen. It could be construed as working illegally.

- Holding a US driver's license and no green card could cause border issues.

- It's important to check out the exact location and the neighborhood, and not just the property itself.

- Some retail locations such as gas stations require a zip code, so Canadian credit cards may not be accepted.

3

Of a Team and a Dream

At work the next day, Ted felt like he had a hangover. His brain hurt and his head was spinning. He wondered if there was such thing as a real estate high, similar to drinking too much where, when you came down from it, all you were left with was a vague recollection of a few conversations and a nagging headache. He had just got back from Phoenix and already the experience was a blur. But Ted wasn't about to give up the real estate rush just yet. He just had to get more information from Sid.

Ted decided to eat lunch at his desk. He set his Tim Hortons coffee and sandwich combo atop a stack of files and took a bite out of an apple fritter before dialing Sid's office number in Toronto. As the phone rang, Ted pulled the Florida flyer from his backpack and set in on his keyboard for inspiration.

Sid picked up on the fourth ring.

"Ted, welcome back. How was the flight? Sorry that house down there didn't work out for you," he said, skipping the customary greeting. "I guess you're not going to be a snowbird after all?"

Ted expected this type of reaction from Sid. After all, the last time they spoke he was devastated, standing on the street in Phoenix in front of the house with the hole blown through it. Ted still couldn't believe that happened to him. But he wasn't going to let one bad experience sidetrack him. He didn't want to miss what he firmly believed could be a great buying opportunity down south right now. He just needed to find the right house, in the right place.

"Well, Sid, I haven't given up. Phoenix was a train wreck, that's for sure, but I've been thinking maybe I just started off on the wrong foot," Ted said as he flipped through the Florida flyer in front of him.

There was a pause on the other end of the line.

"Really, Ted? I thought that experience with that realtor in Arizona put you off for life. You sounded pretty devastated on the weekend there."

"I was put off for a while Sid, but you know, I really think I can make this happen for me. I just need to do a little more homework. You were right about visiting the place myself. I can't thank you enough for that advice. Now, I was thinking maybe I should look somewhere else other than Phoenix, although that's still on my mind. I was thinking maybe Florida. You seem pretty happy with the property you have down there. And you own a few of them if I remember correctly. I don't see why Nancy and I can't retire on the east coast of the US. I always thought Florida was too far, but I'm sure they don't call it the 'world's vacation and retirement destination' for nothing."

Ted heard laughter on the other end of the line.

"I'm not joking, Sid," he said. "In fact, I have an idea."

"Uh-oh," Sid replied. "Not another idea."

"Just hear me out Sid. I'm serious about this. I was thinking that Nancy and I would go to Florida and check out a few places. We've been meaning to take Susie to Disneyland in

California for her tenth birthday, but we could go to Disney World in Florida instead. It's the same thing, I'm sure. And, if you don't mind, we'll take you up on that standing offer of staying with you and Sarah and the kids for a few days at your new place. You're still planning to go down for the holidays, right? We could come after Christmas. What do you think?"

Sid didn't hesitate to reply.

"Ted, it's a great idea. We'd love to have you guys come stay with us; you are welcome any time, of course. But let me ask you: What's the plan for Florida? Are you planning to buy a house and rent it out and retire there later? What's your goal?"

"My goal?" Ted said. "My goal is to find a place to live when I'm old and gray. I have no intention of spending my winters after retirement in the cold and the pouring rain. And if I don't look now it could get too expensive again!"

"Ted, can you hold on a second?" Sid said. "I have to get this other line. Be right back. Don't hang up."

Ted waited patiently for about five minutes until Sid finally returned to the line.

"Sorry, Ted, I had to take that other call. It was urgent."

"No problem," Ted said, slightly irked. "So Nancy and I will start making some plans to come down late next month. Does that work for you?"

"Sounds great, buddy. Tell you what, in the meantime, talk to Nancy about what kind of property you're looking for. Maybe Florida isn't the right place, but you guys should have that conversation. You have to include her. She's your wife, and I know she supports you. She just wants to support the right decision."

"Wow, Sid, is that Sarah talking?" Ted asked.

"Very funny, Ted. I'm serious. You don't want to make this an investment outside the marriage. Do it together. It will be great to see you again, and Nancy and little Susie. I can't believe she's almost 10!"

"I'll talk to Nancy more about it tonight," Ted said. "Talk soon."

"Bye for now, Ted."

Ted finished the apple fritter and licked the sugar glaze off his fingers before flipping the pages of the Florida flyer. He noticed a website for house listings on the back of it, and typed the URL into his work computer. Up popped a dozen or so photos of homes and condominiums for sale across the state, each surrounded by palm trees with descriptions such as "paradise," "walk to the beach," and "relaxing getaway." Ted sat back and daydreamed he was holding a drink beside his backyard pool in Florida after a morning of driving golf balls at the range beside Tiger Woods. He smiled and suddenly felt more confident about his decision to look at buying US property. All he had to do now was warm Nancy to the idea.

BEN & JERRY AND DISNEY WORLD

When Nancy and Susie came through the door at the end of the day, Ted was waiting in the kitchen. He had a dinner of spaghetti and his famous meatball sauce ready on the stove and a carton of Ben & Jerry's Chunky Monkey ice cream in the freezer. Spaghetti is Susie's favorite meal after soccer practice, and ice cream is what Nancy turns to when she is stressed or feels she deserves a special treat. Ted thought it would be best if he had Ben & Jerry on standby tonight.

"Wow, supper is ready?" Nancy asked, "What do you need me to do?"

"Nothing, sweetheart. Just sit down and enjoy. I've done everything."

Nancy glared suspiciously at Ted, while Susie ran up the stairs to her room. Ted shouted to his daughter to be ready in five minutes for dinner.

"It's your favorite!" he hollered up the stairwell.

Nancy was still staring at her husband.

"Okay, Ted. I will eat first but then I want to know what this is all about," said Nancy, always the skeptic.

"I have a great idea Nancy. Wait 'til you hear it. This one you'll really like."

"Should I have a full stomach for this, Ted? Maybe I should skip the meatballs?" Nancy said jokingly.

"My wife the comedian," Ted said, then grabbed her hand and led her to the dining room table. He pulled out a chair and asked her to sit. Susie sprang into the dining room, still dressed in her soccer uniform, her ponytail bouncing behind her.

"Dad bought Chunky Monkey, Mum. I saw it in the freezer," she said with a big grin.

"Oh boy," Nancy said, as Ted served her a helping of meatballs. "Just tell me now. What have you done?"

Ted filled everyone's plates with spaghetti and sauce then sat down and tucked a napkin under the neckline of his shirt. As he twisted a few of noodles around his fork, Ted turned to Susie and said: "Remember how Mom and Dad promised to take you to Disneyland someday? How about Disney World in Florida instead?"

Susie screamed, which forced Nancy to cup her hands over her ears.

"No way! Dad. When?" Susie screeched.

"Yeah, Dad, when?" Nancy asked. She didn't seem as excited.

Ted began to tell Nancy his plan about visiting Sid, Sarah and their kids in Florida, and how it would be a great time to take Susie to Disney World. Nancy sat quietly and listened. There was no expression on her face, but she didn't seem upset, either, so Ted kept talking. He listed the different places they could go from Disney in Orlando to Cape Canaveral. ("It's where the astronauts take off from when they go into space," he explained to Susie, who was more interested in Mickey Mouse.)

Nancy continued to eat slowly as Susie ran off to get the atlas in her room to see where Florida was in relation to Vancouver.

Before Nancy even had a chance to open her mouth, Ted explained: "Okay, okay, I do want to go to Florida, and I do want to take Susie to Disney, but while we're there I think it will be a good chance to look at some real estate. Sid thinks it's a great idea."

Nancy stopped chewing: "Are you mad? Florida is on the other side of the continent. And what do you mean Sid thinks it's a good idea? What about Nancy?"

Susie returned with the atlas. At the same time she flipped it open to the map of Florida, Ted pulled a half-dozen print-outs of property listings from across the state that he found online earlier that day. All of the listings were for places less than US$250,000, Ted said. Some were condos, others town-homes and a few were houses in urban and suburban centers throughout the state. Ted then read from one of the printouts: "The state is leading the nation in tourism, with its year-round sunny climate, swaying palm trees and unique combination of snow-white beaches along the Gulf of Mexico and crashing surf along the Atlantic Coast."

He paused and looked up at his wife.

"How does that sound Nancy? I think we could get used to that kind of life."

Nancy shook her head in disbelief.

"Oh, please Mummy," Susie said, her fingers folded, pleading. "Please say we can go to Disney World. Please!"

"We'll talk about it, Susie. If you're done supper please go to your room and finish your math assignment. I'll come by and check it later. Dad and I need some time to talk now. And leave the atlas; your father is about to get a geography lesson."

As Susie skipped out of the room, listing off the names of the Seven Dwarfs, Nancy turned to Ted and told him to meet her in the living room, with the ice cream.

"Now, I know what you are thinking, Nancy," Ted said after returning from the freezer and handing her the Ben & Jerry's carton and a spoon.

Before he could continue, she cut him off: "Trust me, Ted, you don't know what I'm thinking."

She dug out her first scoop of dessert and told Ted that, in fact, she knew all about his plan to look at property in Florida. "And I'm not upset, if that's what you are thinking," she said.

"What? How?" Ted said.

"That was me on the other line with Sid today," Nancy said.

Ted was stunned.

"We talked on the weekend, after you had that terrible experience in Arizona. I called him again this morning, at the same time you were on the other line asking about Florida, and suggested a trip. He thought I knew about this plan of yours, and was pretty embarrassed when he discovered I didn't. Ted, you have to include me in these plans. Sid and I also agreed that you and I have a lot of thinking to do about this property purchase in the States, if we want to do it together."

Ted was sitting forward on the La-Z-Boy recliner, his elbows resting on his thighs and his head hanging below his shoulders.

Nancy kept on: "We can go to Florida next month; we both have that week off and Susie's out of school and I would love to visit Sid and Sarah in their place down there. As for buying a property, let's make sure it's something that's right for the whole family. I'm not sure Florida is where we want to go, but maybe it is. I haven't been there since I was in my 20s, so let's just go down and take a look and have some fun. But let's do this together from now on, okay? Let's invest in this together."

Ted couldn't believe his ears. He was expecting resistance from Nancy, but she was ready to give it a try. He was sure that once she really thought about it, and saw how inexpensive homes were there, she would be on board.

"This is great! I knew you'd come around!" Ted said. He jumped up from the couch and gave Nancy a kiss on the cheek.

He was as giddy as Susie was when the word Disney came up.

"Not so fast, though, Ted," Nancy said. "Before we do anything, we have to make a plan. We have to figure out what kind of home we're looking at. We need to decide if we want a timeshare—which I'm not sure we do but it's worth looking at—or are we buying something to rent out when we aren't there, or is it just for us for vacations? We also have a ton to learn about all the tax considerations. We have a lot of homework to do, Ted. Speaking of which, I should go help Susie with hers."

This is the Nancy he knew and loved. She was good at being in charge and when she was, life was a lot easier. Ted nodded in agreement at everything she said.

"Tell you what, Ted," Nancy said as she walked out of the living room, "While I'm upstairs helping Susie, you should go online and find us some cheap flights to Tampa. That's where Sid said we should fly into; it's closest to his place. Then, on the weekend, we'll make our list of what we want to do with this home. In the meantime, look at that atlas and remind yourself how far Florida is from Vancouver."

Ted was excited. "You'll thank me for this someday, Nancy. You'll see! When we're 65 and sitting by the pool in our shorts and T-shirts in the middle of winter, you'll thank me."

Ted headed straight for the computer. He first noticed a couple of emails from Sid in his inbox. The first had a list of recommendations on how to find a good realtor, and an article on the pros and cons of buying a foreclosure, tips on how to find foreclosures, and how to do a short sale, which Sid explained is when lenders discount existing loan payoffs. "Hope some of this helps," Sid wrote.

The second email was about another way to buy US property—through a fund, instead of actually buying the bricks and mortar. "Just something else to consider," Sid wrote. "But talk to your financial planner about this if you're even interested."

Ted forwarded the emails to Nancy then flipped over to the travel website to check out flights and prices to Florida in late December.

A PLAN DEVELOPS

On this particular Saturday afternoon, Ted and Nancy carved out a couple hours before dinner to start talking seriously about their potential real estate investment. Nancy had papers spread out on the dining room table, as well as a box that contained their important papers and receipts.

"What do you need that for?" Ted asked, looking at the box.

"First things first, Ted," Nancy said, peering at him over top of her glasses. "We have a few things about this house we need to plan for before we start considering buying another property."

Ted gulped.

"Let me guess. The new roof you keep nagging me about getting. That's $15,000, Nancy. We don't need a new roof yet," Ted said.

"Yes, Ted, this spring we are getting a new roof. If we don't budget for it now, we never will."

"What else?" Ted dared to ask.

Nancy took this rare investment discussion to go over their registered retirement savings plan, their pensions, Susie's education fund and their "rainy day fund," which was three months of living expenses that she insisted be set aside at all times.

"The way I see it, Ted, is that all together we can afford to spend about $250,000 for a property in the States—and that could be as much as $300,000 Canadian depending on where the dollar sits at the time we buy. What we should do is put at least 20 per cent down. We can use equity we've got in our home and arrange for financing in the US for the balance."

Ted was impressed.

"But what we need to figure out first is why we are buying this place. What are we going to use it for?"

"To retire!" Ted said. "That's what I want it for."

"Me too, Ted, but do we want to pick our retirement home now? What we could do is invest in a place and rent it out, hopefully at a monthly profit. We can use that extra money for things like, say, paying for a new roof, or traveling to other parts of the world other than the US."

"Or," Ted interjected, "we could buy a place we like now, rent it out for a few years, then take over that place when we retire."

"We could do that, Ted. But you see, these are the kind of considerations we have to discuss and mull around in our heads before we put our money down on something. It's not only a matter of real estate being cheap. We have to have a bit of a plan," Nancy said.

Ted nodded. He knew she was right, again.

"What I think is that we'll be spending some quality time with Sid next month and we can ask him all sorts of questions like this. He's been through it all before. He has investment properties down there and now his own vacation home. He's an expert, and he's your best friend; you should lean on him for advice."

"Maybe I'm tired of Sid always being the know-it-all," Ted said.

"Maybe instead you should be grateful that he's such a great friend," Nancy replied.

"You're right, of course," Ted acknowledged. "By the way, I think I found us a pretty good deal on some flights. Let me get the information."

Ted rushed off to the other room and Nancy leaned back in her chair and sighed. She was satisfied with how their plan was going, so far. She was also looking forward to spending part of her Christmas vacation in a hot, sunny climate.

NANCY'S CHECKLIST

- Make a plan.
- Never ever buy a house without visiting it at least ONCE and the area at least TWICE!

- Decide where you want to live (exact location can come later).
- Decide what type of property you want. Choices include:
  - Time share. You buy a property that is jointly owned by multiple people and you are allowed to use it only during a specific period each year;
  - Condominium. Similar to condos in Canada, you buy a unit in a building and are subject to condo fees, property taxes, as well as other rules and regulations set out by the building's condo corporation;
  - House or town home. You own the house and the property around it and are subject to property taxes.
- Decide if you're buying an **investment property** or a **vacation property**. If you are buying an investment property, how long do you plan to own it? If you are buying a vacation property, how often do you plan to use it? Or, do you plan to rent it out first, and then live in it down the road.

Why Buy?

Top 10 questions to ask yourself before considering buying real estate in the US:

- Why am I considering a purchase in the US?
- When do I plan to buy, and what is the rationale for my timeframe?
- Is my goal to generate wealth or have a vacation property?

- Do I have a personal and financial plan for the next three to five years? If so, where does this property fit into that plan?
- What size of property do I need?
- What location is the most desirable, based on the information I have now?
- How often will I use this property? For how many days, weeks or months of the year?
- How will I commute to and from this property from my current home?
- Have I done all of the research on the property, such as location, purchase fundamentals and tax implications?
- Am I prepared to lose money on this property, which is a risk with any investment?

Source: Philip McKernan Inc., **www.philipmckernan.com**.

What Are Timeshares?

A timeshare is a form of ownership or right to the use of a property. It is also the term used to describe such properties. Timeshares are typically resort condominium units, in which multiple parties hold rights to use the property, and each sharer is allotted a period of time (typically one week) they may use the property. Timeshares may be on a part-ownership or lease/"right to use" basis, in which the sharer holds no claim to ownership of the property.

The timeshare system is said to have been created in Europe in the 1960s when a ski resort encouraged guests to "stop renting a room" and instead "buy the hotel." Developers worldwide quickly embraced the concept, boosting sales of surplus condominium units at a time when the resort industry was depressed.

Due to the promise of exchange, these units, called "vacation ownership" by the industry, often sell regardless of their deeded resort (most are deeded into a certain resort site, though other forms of use do exist). The vast majority of inventory flows through two international exchange companies: Resort Condominiums International (RCI) and Interval International (II).

This concept has attracted many resort developers and prominent hoteliers, such as Starwood, Wyndham, Hyatt, Hilton, Marriott and Disney.

Source: **www.wikipedia.org**.

4

Of Florida and Mount Everest

At 11 a.m., Ted walked through the kitchen and out onto the deck of Sid's Tampa-area home where Nancy, Susie and Sid's family were relaxing in shorts and T-shirts, finishing breakfast.

"Morning sleepyhead," Nancy said to Ted, still in his pajamas, his hair bristling in several directions.

Sarah rushed over and gave Ted a hug, then handed him a cup of coffee.

"That was quite a flight," Ted said, referring to the trip from Vancouver to Tampa the day before. The plane left Vancouver at 7 a.m. Pacific Time, and arrived at the Tampa airport at 7:30 p.m. Eastern Time. Not only did it take a long time, but also given that it was the week between Christmas and New Year's, the airports were packed. Ted complained about not even being able to sit in the same row as Nancy and Susie on the second of the two flights it took to get there, and spending what seemed like an hour at the Tampa airport waiting for their luggage.

"But we're here now and the weather looks pretty good to me!" Ted said, taking a seat in the sun. "What a place, Sid. How long have you had this, now?"

"It'll be seven years in May. It's been good to us, this house. Lots of good memories so far, and lots more to come."

Ted nodded and looked across Sid's yard at the kidney-shaped pool, the bright green freshly cut grass and the palm trees swaying above.

"What's the plan for today?" Ted asked, looking over at Sid.

"Well, while you were sleeping Nancy, Susie and Sarah already made plans to go shopping. Our kids have already taken off to go waterskiing for the day with some friends. So, that leaves you and me. I thought we could take a drive and I could show you a few neighborhoods around here, if you're interested."

"Sounds great to me," Ted said. "Let me just grab a shower, slap on some sunscreen—which looks like I'll need a lot of today—and I'll be ready to go in a few minutes."

TOP DOWN, EYES OPEN

Ted took the passenger seat in Sid's convertible. As they pulled out of the driveway, Ted was struck by how big the house was from the outside. Driving down the street, Ted felt like he was on a movie set; the clean, wide streets lined with pink and yellow homes and their perfectly manicured lawns. On his right, he saw a golf course, and in the distance, sailboats dotted the bay. As they drove closer to the water, Ted pointed out the window and shouted to Sid: "Are those dolphins?" Sid, who was talking on his cell phone, nodded and continued his telephone conversation.

Ted was in awe. As the warm wind whipped around him, Ted's smile widened. Sid hung up the phone, turned to Ted and said: "So, what do you think?"

"Sid, this is amazing. I love it. I'll take it!"

Sid laughed at his friend's seemingly endless exuberance.

"Tell you what, Ted. Today, I'm going to show you a little more about how you get to a place like this. Maybe it'll help you with your plan to buy someday."

"Sounds good," said Ted.

Sid turned the car left, away from the water and along a busy roadway lined with strip malls, big box stores and apartment buildings. As they drove, Ted noticed the houses were getting smaller and the cars in the driveways older, and there was less greenery than in Sid's neighborhood.

"Where are you taking me?" said Ted, less impressed with the new surroundings.

Sid pulled into the driveway of a townhouse, one of about 40 in the complex. They looked identical. There was a fenced pool and a mattress leaning against a dumpster. A group of teenage boys were shooting hoops at a small park outside, while a gaggle of girls watched from a bench on the sidelines. Someone was painting the outside trim around the windows of one of the townhouses. He waved to Sid, who waved back.

"See this complex here?" Sid said to Ted, pointing to the building in front of them. "I own nine units in it."

Ted looked surprised. "Since when?"

"Well, the first one I bought about 20 years ago, when the savings and loan crisis caused a crash in the real estate market. Then I bought another one two years after that, then a couple more and so on. The first two needed a lot of work. I had them fixed up, new kitchen, bathroom; one needed new carpet and flooring. I have been renting them out ever since. I bought other units as they came up and then renovated them, which helped drive up their value. I waited a few years after each purchase and used the equity from the units I already owned to buy the next ones."

"Are they all in this complex?" Ted asked.

"Yes. I like this location," Sid said. "I know the tenant profile and the area, which is also a big part of buying real estate, as you know. Right, Ted?"

"Right, of course," Ted hesitated.

"And this, Ted, is how I raised the money to buy my own place down here. It took a long time. But I planned for it. It was also a lot of work and a lot of trips back and forth from Toronto—which wasn't so bad, especially during the winter. Although the travel costs can really add up, so you have to be careful."

Ted looked thoughtful. He had no idea Sid had been in the real estate game for so long.

"Wow, Sid, that's impressive. I don't doubt it's been a lot of work."

"But it's like working for yourself, so it's a different type of work," Sid said. "You know that what you put into it you can get out of it, threefold, if you're smart about it. I wasn't at first. The first four or five units I bought were tough going at times and I made mistakes. That said, I had a goal—to have a place of my own—and I never lost sight of that. It got easier the more I learned, and experienced how it all works—the taxes, rental income, renovations. I don't think everyone has to do it the way I did, Ted, but I wanted to show you how I've done it. This is how I was finally able to buy my own home down here in a neighborhood I desired. I've been investing down here for a long time. And, like I said, I made a lot of mistakes. That might be why I am being a bit hard on you Ted. I want to help you avoid making the mistakes I made."

"But Sid, I don't want to wait decades," Ted said. "And from what you've just showed me, it looks like I missed the boat."

Sid shook his head in disagreement.

"Listen, you are getting old, Ted—and, by the way, you are definitely aging faster than me," Sid teased, "but it's never too late to start. You know the old Chinese proverb: 'The best time to plant a tree is 20 years ago. The second best is today.'"

Ted was not impressed with the poke about his age, but was intrigued by Sid's investment strategy. Was he ready for that much work? Sid also had years of experience doing this, but Ted didn't want to wait that long. Maybe he and Nancy should just buy a house and rent it out until they're ready to move in when they retire. Ted suddenly realized why everyone keeps talking to him about "The Plan."

"Let's get some lunch and you can tell me more about how you did this. I want to hear about the first time you bought. What you learned that you didn't know before. Then how about we hit a driving range," Ted suggested to Sid.

The friends hopped back in the car. As they drove off, Ted looked at Sid's building through the rearview mirror. He had a lot to think about.

"I like that tree quote, Sid," Ted said. "It makes me feel better about what I haven't done in my life so far, and I'm not just talking real estate."

WIDE WORLD OF DISNEY

On their second day in Florida, Ted and Nancy planned to take Susie to Disney World. They rented a car and began the 90-minute journey from Sid's house. As they drove, Ted told Nancy about Sid's investment property and said it would not be too late for them.

"You know, Nancy, it's never too late to plant a tree," Ted said.

"What do trees have to do with anything, Ted?" Nancy said, looking confused.

"Never mind," Ted replied, as he fiddled with the cruise-control button.

"I'm not sure that's our thing, buying a bunch of units and renovating them and renting them out," said Nancy. "But I'm really glad he showed it to you. I still think we have a lot to learn before we buy. I'm also not sure yet if this is the right state for us. It's beautiful, but that flight is not something I'd want to do more than once a year. We're not getting any younger either, Ted. Retirement is still 15 or 20 years away. That's a lot of trips."

"I know, Nancy. There's a lot to consider. Let's just see everything we can while we're down here, and try to have some fun."

As they pulled into the Magic Kingdom parking lot at Disney World, Susie had her face pressed against the window from inside the air-conditioned car. She was looking for Mickey Mouse or Minnie, anything beyond a sea of cars that proved they were there, at last.

The three of them spent most of the day in lineups for rides, eating junk food and soaking up the cartoon atmosphere. Around late afternoon, Ted spotted a huge lineup in front of a building with a sign that read: Disney Vacation Club.

"Hey, Nancy. Check this out. It's that timeshare program we were reading about in that magazine on the plane. Let's see what it's all about."

"Do we want a timeshare, Ted?"

"Probably not, but we're here, so why not just go in and check it out. It'll be fun. I bet even Susie will like it."

Susie, who had been powered by sugar for most of the day, nodded her head furiously. They took their place in yet another line, waiting for their turn to tour the so-called "Disney Dream Experience." As they walked through the front entrance, Ted felt like he had entered a high-end hotel, the kind he couldn't afford. They were greeted by a cheery registration clerk named Bill, who signed them in, gave them nametags and invited them to sit in the reception area. It was well stocked with desserts. Susie grabbed a giant cookie covered in Smarties, and even before they had a chance to sit, they were greeted by another enthusiastic Disney staffer named Steve.

"So, where are you from?" Steve asked with a wide grin.

"Vancouver," Ted replied.

"The Olympics, right?" Steve said. "Beautiful place. I've seen pictures. But cold in the winter, I bet. I'm originally from Chicago. I know cold. That's why you're here?"

Ted nodded in agreement and Nancy smiled politely as Steve began to explain how the Disney Vacation Club worked.

"You buy points that can be used to stay in any of their destinations around the world," Steve explained. He also said there were specific packages that allowed you to take advantage of certain destinations, and the price often depended on when you wanted to go. Buyers received a deed at the time of purchase that could be sold at any time, he said. When Steve finished his pitch, he took the family to see one of the units.

As they entered the space, Ted immediately noticed how small it was, albeit cozy. As they walked towards the window to check the view, Susie gasped, pointed outside and then jumped up and down repeatedly.

"Look, Dad, you can see the castle from here!" she said excitedly.

Ted looked out the window and noticed that, indeed, the unit had a stunning view of the theme park.

"Pretty impressive," Ted said, looking over at Nancy, who said nothing. Ted took this as a sign that she had no intention of buying here and was not about to give Steve any indication otherwise. Ted knew Nancy had seen enough. As Steve continued to describe the features of the unit, Ted stopped him mid-sentence. He then held out his hand to signal it was time for them to leave.

"I think we've taken up enough of your time," Ted said, then shook Steve's hand. "This is not for us, but thank you for your hospitality."

Steve accepted defeat on that potential sale and watched Ted and his family walk out without another word.

As they headed back out into the sunshine and heard the roar of roller coasters overhead, Ted turned to Susie and said: "Mom and Dad just wanted to see what it would be like, but we'll find something even better than this. We promise."

Nancy nodded.

Ted asked: "How about we catch that Nemo show now, Susie? What do you say?"

Both Nancy and Susie agreed and the three marched back into the depths of the theme park to find Nemo.

FLORIDA'S SPACE COAST

After two days of Disney theme parks, Ted and Nancy were looking forward to a change of pace. Their plan was to spend the day with Sid and Sarah visiting attractions such as the Kennedy Space Center and the US Astronaut Hall of Fame, while Susie hung out with Sid's teenagers at the beach. Ted also wanted to visit a couple of condo complexes along the route, even though Nancy was growing more skeptical of buying anything in Florida.

"It's just too far for us to come, I think," Nancy said when Sid asked for her thoughts in the car on the drive to Cape Canaveral.

"I can see what you mean," Sid replied. "We're in Toronto, so it's a lot closer. Usually Canadians buy sunbelt property more directly south from where they live. But I do know a guy who has property down here who lives in Calgary, and he loves it. Everyone is different."

"Maybe we'll buy one here and one in Arizona. That way we'll have the ocean and the desert," Ted said from the back seat. Sarah, who was sitting beside him, waited for Nancy's cue before laughing.

"It's a joke, Nancy," Ted said. "Or maybe it isn't. Maybe someday we will have both. That's why I'm so convinced the time to buy is now. The prices can only really go up from here, even if they go down a little bit more, they can't stay this low forever. Besides, there will be so many of us Baby Boomers begging for vacation property in a few years, we want to pick the best ones now. After all, Sid, this is where you recommend we invest, right?"

"Wrong," Sid shot back instantly. "It's all about what works for you and if it fits your . . ."

"Let me guess: 'My plan,'" Ted shouted back.

Sarah picked up where Sid left off: "You can invest in many places across the US no matter what the market is doing. This country is so big that there are always good properties to buy for investment, but you need to know what you're looking for."

Sid continued: "Tomorrow, Ted, I'm going to introduce you to my friend Garth. He has a place down the bay from us. He bought it with another couple. He has a great place and can tell you how they make it work. He's taking us out on his boat, if you're up for it. The kids can hang out with Susie again tomorrow for a few hours while we head out. How does that sound?"

"Sounds great," Nancy said.

"Works for me," Ted agreed.

"Speaking of 'boats,' Ted," Sid said with a mischievous grin.

"Ha, ha, isn't Sid funny," Ted said sarcastically, causing everyone to break out in laughter.

As they traveled down the coast towards the space center, Ted noticed an open house sign on a complex overlooking the ocean.

"Hey, Sid, can we stop here? Let's check it out. We have a few minutes, don't we?"

"I don't mind, if you ladies don't mind," said Sid.

Nancy and Susan both agreed to stop. Sid pulled over and made a U-turn back to the development.

"It looks brand new," said Sid. "Pretty nice spot."

As they pulled up to the main entrance, they noticed there were no cars in the parking lot.

"Looks pretty desolate," said Sid. "Sign of the times, I guess?"

As they stepped out of the car, a man with a white dress shirt, khaki pants and shiny brown shoes walked towards them.

"Welcome. Are you here for the open house?" he said.

"Yes, we are," said Sid, shaking the man's hand. "We were just driving by and noticed this beautiful spot. Can you show us around a bit?"

"Sure can. My name is Joseph, and this is my property. I developed it. Everything is top-of-the-line; only the best quality materials were used. Come on in and we'll have a quick chat and I'll show you some of the units for sale."

Ted and Nancy, Sid and Sarah followed Joseph to a bright spacious office at the front of the complex, which faced the ocean. There was a strong wind blowing, which amplified the sound of the ocean waves crashing against the shore. It was so loud, in fact, that Ted could barely make out Joseph's lengthy description of the complex. It brought back memories of Phoenix and the deafening sound of the fighter jets flying above. Ted laughed to himself; it was obvious the sound of ocean waves were much more soothing.

After a quick chat inside Joseph's office, the couples learned that he was a retired developer who took on this project about five years ago. It was his last development, his swan song before retiring to his own home up the coast. As Joseph was explaining the community to Sarah and Nancy, Sid leaned over to Ted and whispered: "I bet Joseph would already be retired and living in that big house if it weren't for this noose around his neck."

"What do you mean?" said Ted.

"I mean, this place is empty," Sid said. "It's gorgeous, and you can see the quality workmanship, but nobody is buying these units. Who has $850,000 to spend on a condo these days? Not a lot of people. Why do you think he's the one showing us around? Normally they hire people to do that."

Ted began to understand more about the diversity of the US real estate market. Even the best-built homes in the most beautiful locations were having trouble selling. On the one hand, it was a shame, Ted thought. On the other hand, it made for another good excuse to buy something soon, especially given the wide selection.

"Sid, Ted, come over here and let me show you something amazing about these units," Joseph said.

He led them towards a unit that was closest to the water. It had a 180-degree view of nothing but ocean, beach and blue sky.

"It looks beautiful now, doesn't it?" Joseph said.

Ted and Sid nodded in agreement.

"But when those hurricanes come, it can get pretty ugly. That's why I had these windows installed. They are hurricane proof," said Joseph, and then he struck the glass a few times with his fist.

"Is that even possible?" Ted asked. "Don't you have to board them up anyway?"

"Ted, my friend, let me tell you about these windows. If a two-by-four came flying at these windows at 150 miles an hour, they wouldn't shatter. These are the best windows you could ever own, especially here."

Ted noticed how proud Joseph was of this place he'd created. He also felt pity. If what Sid said was true, Joseph should be relaxing on his patio right now, not standing here trying to sell them a house on his own. They were not going to buy, and Joseph likely knew it. Not only was this place out of Ted's price range and too far away, but also the "hurricane factor" wasn't something he was prepared to deal with. He had a flashback of stories he'd seen on CNN about residents boarding up their homes and fleeing for shelter inland. Vancouver was just too far away to handle issues like that when they come up, Ted thought.

He then turned to Sid. "I've seen enough. We can go anytime you're ready."

Sid agreed it was time to leave, and he went to gather Nancy and Sarah, who were standing and chatting under a palm tree, admiring the ocean view.

Ted then thanked Joseph for the tour.

"Great place. Great job. I think it's a bit beyond our price range, unless you want to chop those asking prices by 60 per cent or more," Ted said, laughing.

"Oh, I wish I could," said Joseph. "I've already dropped the price three times. But if you want to write me an offer I will look at it seriously."

Ted declined graciously. "Sorry, Joseph. I wish you the best of luck. It's a wonderful development in a beautiful spot."

Joseph put both of his hands around Ted's right hand and gave it a gentle shake.

"I appreciate you stopping by to visit," Joseph said. "It's my pleasure to show you around. Tell your friends about my place. Tell them to call me any time."

Joseph then gave Ted his business card, which had an office number, cell phone number and beeper.

"That's a lot of numbers," Ted said, looking down at the card.

"Call any time my friend," Joseph said.

Ted tucked the card in his wallet and walked back to the car where Sid and the others were waiting.

"Beautiful place," said Nancy. "I hope he sells something soon."

Sid pulled back out on the highway and Joseph watched from the side of the road as the car sped away towards Port Canaveral.

GREETING GARTH

On Ted and Nancy's last full day in Florida, Sid took them to meet his friend Garth, who lived in an older two-bedroom condo complex in a gated community overlooking a golf course near Tampa. Garth and his wife had purchased it with another couple five years ago.

The layout reminded Ted of the set of that once-popular television show Melrose Place, with a pool in the center of the complex and the units built in a circle around it. He imagined the drama that might unfold between the unit owners and late night rendezvous. He joked about this with Garth, who promised the building was nothing like *Melrose Place*.

"In fact, I think most of the owners are over the age of 55," said Garth, as they stood on the deck overlooking the 13th hole. "I'd say we are the youngest owners in the building."

"Why did you buy in this spot?" Ted asked.

Garth explained that he and his wife, and the other couple they bought with, chose it because they wanted a place they could afford and that other people would want to rent.

"Serious renters, people you would trust when you live thousands of miles away, want a quiet environment like this," said Garth.

And while none of the four owners are avid golfers, Garth said they chose the golf course location because short-term renters were interested in a property with a view of a golf course or the water.

"The water view was a lot more expensive, so this works wonderfully," Garth said.

"In fact, I love sitting out here. Even though I don't golf much, I find it very peaceful."

Ted was curious how Garth made this all work when he shared the condo with another couple, and they rented it out.

"When do you use it? When do others? Who figures it out?" Ted asked. Nancy, who came along with Sid and Ted to meet Garth, was also curious about renting vacation property. She sat down beside Ted to hear Garth's reply.

"We pick weeks of the year when we want to be here alone, weeks we want to be here with our co-owners—usually during

March Break and over the Christmas holidays—and the rest of the year we rent it out," Garth said. "But after we bought it, we noticed the rental weeks are the same weeks we want to use it. We made a mistake and regret not knowing that. We have regular yearly renters now, but it didn't start off that way. In fact, it took years to build up what I call our clientele. And sometimes we still fall short."

Garth explained that they began using a property manager to help rent and clean the units. As the years passed, they've been able to do most of the renting themselves, and pay someone to clean the place regularly and check for damage and any other potential issues.

"What about costs like renovations and buying furniture, who pays for that?" asked Nancy. She was also curious to know how many weeks they use the unit, compared to the renters.

"All good questions," said Garth. He explained the costs were split evenly between the two couples—everything from fixing the sink to painting the ceiling. Both couples spent about four weeks a year at the complex, two of them together, for a total of six weeks, and rented it out the rest of the year.

Garth pointed out that with a condo, as opposed to owning a house, the outside of the building is always maintained by the condo corporation. This removes some of the worry of owning when you live in another country.

"I get some peace of mind from that," he said.

Nancy was captivated by the conversation and asked Garth to explain, in hindsight, what they would have done differently.

"Anybody buying a property down here should do more research than we did, because there are different tax implications," said Garth. "The taxes also differ depending on what state you buy in."

Garth said they bought in Florida, but also considered Arizona, and that taxes in these two states are different.

"I almost bought a place in Arizona!" Ted piped up. "It was a house but it had a few problems, so I backed out."

Sid burst out laughing. "That's an understatement. It was a war zone!"

Ted gave Sid a dirty look. "Forget him. Tell me, Garth, why did you choose Florida instead?"

Garth explained that his partners in the condo were from Ottawa and they preferred Florida. What's more, his wife was from Halifax, where her parents and sister live, so having a place in Florida made the most sense, especially given that it was a shared purchase.

"Do you mind telling us what the value is now?" Ted asked.

Garth smiled. "From when we bought it to the peak around 2006, it nearly doubled. Today, I think it would be worth closer to what we picked it up for."

"Too bad you didn't sell it at the peak," Ted said. "Do you regret that?"

"Ted!" shouted Nancy, appalled by her husband's question.

"It's okay, I don't mind," Garth replied. "You know what, Ted, it was a lifestyle purchase, so the value doesn't matter as much. Now, if I had bought it purely as an investment, I would be concerned."

"I would be sick," Ted replied.

"That's something you have to be prepared for if you're an investor," Sid said. "The value could go down. That's why you want to be a longer-term investor. You want to have . . ."

"I know, Sid—a plan," Ted interrupted. "Hey, Garth, mind if I grab another beer from the fridge?"

"Be my guest."

"Bring me one, too," Sid said.

Nancy also requested a refill from Ted, then kept the conversation going by asking Garth if he felt pressure to use the place each time they go on vacation.

"I would imagine that, given how much time, energy and money you have invested, you would feel compelled to keep coming back. But what if you want to go to Hawaii, instead?" she asked.

"Funny you should say that, Nancy," Garth said. "My wife and I were just talking about that. For sure, you do feel you need to use the property, and my wife loves visiting new and exciting places, so I guess it's a drawback. Our friends go to Maui every year and we always bow out to come here. If I was to do it over, I might have waited and traveled a little more to other places and then spent more time here."

Ted returned to the deck with the beer just as Sid stepped back into the house to take a phone call. Ted and Nancy asked Garth more questions about the renters they've had over the years, and the problems they've encountered.

"It took some getting used to, but my best advice would be to get references for your renters and make friends with your neighbors. They will help look after your place while you're away, just to keep an eye on it. We've made a few friends from within the complex. One couple even came to visit us in Calgary one summer during the stampede."

Ted stood up to stretch and then stared out at the greenery of the golf course before him.

"Garth, you have been really helpful," he said. "I think what you've done is smart. Good for you."

Garth thanked Ted for the compliment as Sid stepped back onto the deck and rejoined the conversation.

"So, Ted, what do you think?" Sid asked.

"I was just telling Garth that I admire what he's done. Sounds like an interesting way to get into the market. It might be a good option for Nancy and me to consider."

"I'm glad the two of you could find time to talk," Sid said. "How about we continue this conversation on the water? Garth, let's take that boat of yours out. What do you say?"

Garth grabbed the keys and slipped on his flip-flops. As they headed out the door, Garth turned to Ted: "That's another thing, Ted, I wouldn't be able to buy a boat down here if I didn't co-own this place. It's the best of both worlds, and even better for my bank account."

That really inspired Ted. He turned to Nancy and said: "What do you think?"

"Well, first, I say 'no' to another boat. But I like that we're learning more about the options. We still have a lot to talk about, but it sounds better every day," she said.

Ted felt lucky they got some first-hand experience on buying property in the US. He also noticed Nancy had become more relaxed about the idea. He put his arm around her shoulder and gave her a kiss on the cheek.

"Thanks, Nancy. Thanks for making all this happen."

The two held hands as they followed Garth and Sid on the short walk to the nearby marina.

TED'S PLAN

On their last night in Florida, Sid, Ted and their families gathered for dinner on the heated patio of a local seafood restaurant surrounded by a dock lined by dozens of houseboats.

"Hey Nancy, maybe we can just buy something like this and live on the water," Ted said and pointed to the boats.

Nancy, who was in deep discussion with Sarah about the differences between the US and Canadian health care systems, looked over at her husband, said "No" and continued on with her conversation. Susie and Sid's two teenagers were at the end of the table comparing music video collections on their iPods.

"See that Sid? No respect," said Ted.

They both laughed. "Hey Sid, how about you tell me more about that deal I heard you discussing earlier today? You buying another property?"

"Yes, a condo in Toronto. I bought it for Sarah and I to move into in a few years, when the kids move out. We want to downsize. It's a building we've been admiring for years."

"Good for you, Sid. But I didn't know you were thinking of moving."

"Not for a few years yet, but a unit in this building came open that we really wanted. It's on the top floor and has a gorgeous view, so we went for it. I found out today the sellers accepted our offer. We close in 60 days."

"Congratulations, Sid," said Ted. "I'm really impressed with how you set these goals, and then you achieve them. I don't know if I have that kind of discipline."

"Sure you do, Ted. Anyone does. You just have to know what your goals are. Take my life for instance. I knew when Sarah and I got married in our 20s that we eventually wanted a house in Florida someday, but we were too young and too busy building our careers and family to buy a vacation home and start using it. So, we decided to buy a place we could rent out—the one in that complex I showed you earlier this week. Then, I slowly worked towards buying the others. I had a plan, a goal in mind, and worked towards it. It's kind of like going on a diet . . ."

"Wait a minute, hold on there," Ted said. "This isn't some lecture to try to put me on a diet is it?"

Ted turned to Nancy, interrupting her conversation again. "Did you guys talk about this, too? I have put on a few pounds since college, but I'm in good shape!"

Ted rubbed his stomach.

Nancy and Sid looked at each other and laughed.

"No, Ted. It's not like *you* trying to lose weight, it's like anyone who says they want to do something, but they haven't thought about how to do it. For me, investing is a long-term strategy. To me, flipping doesn't work. It's like diets. Instead of going on a diet, you have to change your lifestyle, your eating habits and exercise regime. Those are the only diets that ever work in the long run. Real estate for me is the same."

"I still don't get it—the real estate part," Ted said, confused. "I know you have to plan, but what if an opportunity comes along that's just too good to pass up? Like that condo you just bought in Toronto?"

"I wouldn't do it unless I was ready," Sid said. "There's always a deal out there Ted, but you have to be prepared to take it on; otherwise it could backfire. We couldn't have bought that condo in Toronto if we hadn't already done years of prep work, investing and building wealth from these other properties."

As Ted spoke, three waiters delivered meals to the table. Ted ordered another round of drinks and asked Sid to continue with his story as the others began eating.

"Ted, let me ask you a question," Sid said, laying a napkin across his lap. "If you wanted to climb Mount Everest, what's the first thing you'd do if you were standing at the bottom?"

Ted paused, and after about 20 seconds said, "Well, I guess you would take the first step."

"Okay, and after that?" Sid said.

"I guess the next step and keep going."

"All the way to the top?" Sid asked.

"Well, yeah," said Ted with confidence.

"Well, Ted, that's impossible and no human on the planet could do that."

Ted looked stumped.

Sid explained that first, to climb the world's biggest mountain, you need to be both mentally and physically prepared. You also need to pick a team to help you along the journey. You need to prepare your supplies and plan the route before you take your first step. This is all done at base camp, and when you're ready, you start your climb.

"That makes sense. So buying real estate is like climbing Mount Everest?" Ted asked.

"Any goal is like climbing a mountain, Ted, but you don't have to start with Everest. Think about it. If you wanted to climb Everest, you would start by practicing on smaller hills, then mountains and so on until you were ready for the big one. Maybe you've climbed your Everest or maybe it's ahead of you. That's the point. I mean, look at all the mountains you've climbed in your life so far. There's your career, your life with Nancy and how well you've raised Susie. Those are all goals you set for yourself."

Ted nodded, as he began to understand.

Sid continued.

"After you hit camp one, you rest and head for camp two. You acclimatize to the surroundings, and look back at what you've achieved so far. What do you do then, Ted?" Sid asked.

"Well, I guess now that you're rested, you go for camp three," Ted replied, feeling like he was back at school.

"No," Sid said. "You return to base camp."

Ted shook his head. "No wonder it takes so long to climb those damn mountains. I just figured it got tougher—and slower—as you climbed higher."

"Even the fittest and most prepared mountain climbers have to go back and forth to acclimatize properly. In fact, when you finally set out from camp four, the final camp, for the summit, you need oxygen to get to the top. You can't do it alone. You see, Ted, the climb is only part of it; the preparation and patience is what it's all about."

Nancy interjected: "I think what Sid is hinting at, Ted, is that we have to be prepared to take on a huge project, such as climbing a mountain or making a huge investment decision like buying US property. We have to consider more than just the price and the city where we want to buy, but stand back and consider *why* we are buying. How that fits into a larger plan. We have a lot of homework to do, Ted."

Ted knew the vacation was officially over when Nancy started talking about them doing homework.

"Remember that boat you bought Ted?" Sid asked, only this time he wasn't joking.

"Why is everyone picking on me?" Ted asked.

"Ted, I'm serious," Sid continued. "You lost what—$5,000 on that boat? If you buy the wrong property, or more importantly buy any property for the wrong reason, it will cost you way more than that."

Ted nodded in agreement.

A waiter then stopped by the table and handed out dessert menus.

"We will work it all out," Ted said, and then put his arm around his wife. He raised his glass and looked around the table at his family and friends.

"Everyone, I would like to propose a toast to Sid—my friend who once again has shown me the way! Only this time he's conspiring with my wife!"

Everyone laughed and clinked their glasses. "To Sid!"

Florida Weather and Seasons

Florida is known around the world for its balmy weather. The state's mild winters have made it a haven for retirees. Summers can be long and hot with showers providing much appreciated relief during the rainy season. Coastal areas also experience gentle breezes during the summer.

Average Annual Temperatures:
Summer:
80.5 (F) degrees (26.9 C) (North Florida)
82.7 (F) degrees (28.2 C) (South Florida)
Winter:
53.0 (F) degrees (11.7 C) (North Florida)
68.5 (F) degrees (20.3 C) (South Florida)

The six-month hurricane season runs from June 1 through November 30, and Floridians have learned to be ready when a storm threatens the area. More Information: National Hurricane Center: http://www.nhc.noaa.gov/

Tree planting season in Florida (December to February)

Other Interesting Florida Facts

Number of major commercial airports: 19

Number of international airports: 12

Number of deepwater ports: 14

Kilometers of sand beaches: 1,900

Kilometers of coastline: 2,900

Number of golf courses: more than 1,250

Florida has more golf courses than any other state.

Palm Beach County has more golf courses than any other county in the US.

There is no official designation of a "State Motto." The motto "In God We Trust" is widely used but has never been formally adopted by the Florida Legislature.

Sources: **www.stateofflorida.com** compiled using data from: Florida Dept. of State; Visit Florida; U.S. Census Bureau; Bureau of Economic & Business Research (University of Florida); State of **Florida.com research**.

Economy Strengths

- International trade: 40% of all US exports to Latin and South America passes through Florida.
- Tourism: With 76.8 million visitors in 2004 (a record number), Florida is the top travel destination in the world. The tourism industry has an economic impact of $57 billion on Florida's economy.
- Space industry: This represents $4.5 billion of the state's economy. The Kennedy Space Center employs about 15,000 people and Florida ranks fourth among

the states in overall aerospace employment, with 23,000 jobs.

- Agriculture: Florida leads the southeast in farm income. The state produces about 75% of the US oranges and accounts for about 40% of the world's orange juice supply.
- Construction: This industry's strength results from the steady stream of new residents and visitors welcomed to Florida each year.
- Services: Growth in high-tech, financial and back-office operations.
- Software: Many small, entrepreneurial companies.
- Health technology: Medical, biotech, laboratories.
- University research: More than $500 million per year in sponsored research at Florida universities.

Sources: **www.stateofflorida.com** compiled using data from: Florida Dept. of State; Visit Florida; US Census Bureau; Bureau of Economic & Business Research (University of Florida); State of **Florida.com research**.

Florida Facts and Trivia

- Greater Miami is the only metropolitan area in the United States whose borders encompass two national parks. You can hike through pristine Everglades National Park or ride on glass-bottom boats across Biscayne National Park.
- Saint Augustine is the oldest European settlement in North America.

- Florida is not the southernmost state in the US; Hawaii is farther south.
- The *Benwood*, on French Reef in the Florida Keys, is known as one of the most dived shipwrecks in the world.
- The United States city with the highest rate of lightning strikes per capita is Clearwater.
- Gatorade was named for the University of Florida Gators where the drink was first developed.
- Miami Beach pharmacist Benjamin Green invented the first suntan cream in 1944. He accomplished this by cooking cocoa butter in a granite coffee pot on his wife's stove.
- Key West has the highest average temperature in the United States.
- The Saint John's River is one of the few rivers that flows north instead of south.
- In May 1970, Florida lawmakers passed and sent to the Governor a bill adopting the moonstone as the official state gem. Ironically, the moonstone is not found naturally in Florida . . . nor is it found on the moon.
- In 1987, the Florida legislature designated the American alligator (*Alligator mississippiensis*) the official state reptile. Long an unofficial symbol of the state, the alligator originally represented Florida's extensive untamed wilderness and swamps.
- Miami installed the first automated teller bank machine, especially for rollerbladers.
- A swamp such as the Fakahatchee Strand in the Everglades functions in three major ways. First, its

vegetation serves as a filter to clean the water as it makes its slow journey southward. Second, it's a major habitat for wildlife and plant life. Finally, it actually prevents flooding by slowing the flow of water after heavy rains.

- Fort Lauderdale is known as the Venice of America because the city has 185 miles of local waterways.
- Islamorada is billed as the Sports fishing Capital of the World.
- Florida is the only state that has two rivers both with the same name. There is a Withlacoochee in north central Florida (Madison County) and a Withlacoochee in central Florida. They have nothing in common except the name.

Source: **http://www.50states.com/facts/florida.htm**.

SID'S TIPS

- When considering which city to buy in, take into consideration travel time and costs to and from your property, including transportation to and from the airport and length of the flight (including potential stopovers).

- Time zones are an important consideration when buying south of 49.

- If desired, consider buying property with another investor. Factors include splitting costs and responsibilities. The shared property should also be properly drawn out in all legal documents, including each owner's will and estate planning.

- Establish goals for your property purchases. These can include, among other options:
  1. Buying a rental property and using the cash flow for vacations or to build wealth for other properties
  2. Buying a lifestyle property, but renting it out for the first few years, depending on your circumstances, then moving in when you are ready.
  3. Buying the lifestyle property and keeping it for your own year-round use, but making sure you know the true annual carrying costs.
- Ensure your property goals also meet your personal and family goals in the short and long term.

5

Of Experts and Equity

Ted stood in front of the departures screen at the Denver International Airport and saw the word "Canceled" beside a number of flights, including the one he, Nancy and Susie were to take to Vancouver. On the first leg of the trip, from Tampa to Denver, they were warned that a blizzard had blown in and that many flights were already grounded.

"We should have taken that Houston-Seattle connection instead," Ted said to Nancy, whose face was a bit sunburned from their time in Florida. She also looked worn out.

"Maybe. But how were we to know there would be a snow-storm? Besides, the trip has already run to nine hours and that connection would have added at least another couple hours to the journey," Nancy said. Susie was standing beside her, unfazed by the delay. Instead, she was mesmerized by the cavernous Denver airport terminal and the view of the snow piling up outside. She tugged on Nancy's sleeve and begged for them to find a restaurant and eat.

Ted sighed. "Well, we could be stuck in worse places. This airport is huge! Fifty-three square miles, the biggest in North America and the longest runway, three miles long. I read about it on the plane. We should take a look around, get some dinner and wait it out. What choice do we have?"

They walked through the vast terminal, past parts of the public art collection and through a few shops, keeping an eye on the arrivals boards, their fingers crossed that the storm would soon pass.

After walking for about 15 minutes, Susie noticed a lineup in front of a booth where they were handing out stuffed teddy bears. "Can we go there?" she whined. As they approached the booth to see what the giveaway was about, Ted noticed it was people applying for a credit card.

"This is what they're lined up for? A credit-card application?" he asked.

"Can we get one?" Susie asked.

"No, Susie, we don't need another one of those," Ted explained. "And you don't need another stuffed animal."

"Wow," said Nancy. "I don't think I've ever seen a lineup for credit cards before, and certainly never at the airport. Every time we walk by that one at the Vancouver airport it's empty. It's no wonder there are such serious credit problems in America."

They walked past the booth and continued through the terminal until they eventually spotted a steak restaurant that fulfilled Ted's craving for red meat.

"Let's eat here," Ted said, and they settled in for dinner. Ted ordered a steak sandwich and a beer; Nancy chose a grilled chicken salad and Suzie a grilled cheese sandwich with fries and a Coke. As they dug into their meals, Nancy turned to Ted with that "time to talk" look he knew so well.

SETTING GOALS

"Now's probably a good a time as any to start talking about what we want to do next," Nancy said, as Ted carved off another piece of steak sandwich.

"What do you think, Ted? What do we *want* with this property? What are our goals?"

Ted sat quietly for a moment. "I knew you'd hit me with these goals, but I thought it could at least wait until we were home, Nancy."

She looked at Ted and smiled. This was her way of appeasing him, but he knew it didn't mean he was off the hook, either.

"Okay. My goals," Ted began. "Well, first we both know that I got caught up in the emotion of buying in the US and all the hype around buying something now. After talking more with Sid, I realize I was being foolish, and I'm sorry about that. I also should have talked to you more about it before putting that deposit down in Phoenix."

Nancy looked at Ted with a forgiving smile. "I know you meant well," she said, touching his forearm. "Let's focus on the future. So tell me, what do you want this property for? How do you want to do it?"

"Well," Ted paused, putting down his fork and wiping his mouth with a napkin. "I would say that my goal is to have a place of our own someday in the US. Somewhere hot and sunny when it's cold and rainy at home. I think we should buy it sooner, rather than later because the prices are good and there's a huge selection. I see us using it for vacations in the winter. Maybe we could rent it out the rest of the year. But when we're retired, I don't want to have to worry about renting it out when we aren't there. I don't want to worry about renters when I'm 70. I want to worry about not being late for my tee-off time."

"Okay, and how about when we are going to retire?" Nancy asked. "Are we still planning to do that when you turn 60, because that's about 15 years from now, and I'll be 62. What do you think? Is that still the timeline we're working towards?"

Ted sighed. "Well, 'Freedom 55' is definitely out, but I think we can definitely slow down at 60 or a few years after that. What I'd really like to do when we do retire is live in the US place for half the year and stay home the other half. I recall Sid telling me there are rules about how long you can live down there without being considered a taxpaying citizen. Also, I love Vancouver summers and all of our friends are there. We could rent out the US home for the other six months, but I don't want it to break us if we can't find tenants. It should be like extra cash for us if we do, you know, so I can go double or nothing on poker nights."

"Very funny, sweetie, but remember what Garth said. It was his plan to rent it out for a period of time, but during the hot summers who will want to rent it?" Nancy pointed out. "By the way, I can see you already, all gray-haired with your sunhat, floral shirt and your poker chips! Seriously, what about other properties? Do you think we should buy one property, then try to buy others using the cash earned from it?"

Ted sipped his beer and looked up at the football game on the big-screen TV in the restaurant. His eyes then turned back to Nancy and her serious expression.

"I'm not sure I'm the same type of investor Sid is," Ted said. "We could sure use the extra cash he rakes in, but maybe all we want is one place. That's enough hassle for me. I know he's done well by it, but I think we should stay small. One place and if, down the road, we want to upgrade or buy a second property, that's great. But I don't think I'm the real estate tycoon Sid is. I don't think that's us. Besides, he started a lot sooner than we did."

Nancy appeared relieved. "I agree completely. Personally, I really think we should think about buying a place to rent out first. We could play landlord for five years or so, and then use any proceeds for vacations, or to save for our own vacation property some day. I'm not sure I want to vacation in just one place for the rest of my life at this stage. And I definitely think we need to pick something to buy that's on our own side of the continent."

"You mean this airport layover isn't your favorite part of the trip?" Ted smiled. He acknowledged Florida was too far for them.

Nancy continued, again reminding Ted of Sid's friend Garth in Florida. He bought with friends and it took them a few years to get a good rental routine happening.

"I don't know anyone we could buy with," Nancy said, "or anyone I would want to share an investment with. I would rather we do it on our own, at our own pace."

Ted liked what Nancy was saying. Meantime, Susie was listening carefully to her parents' conversation, trying to figure out what it all meant.

"Does this mean we are moving to the US?" she asked. "I don't want to move. I won't have any friends and I like my friends at home, and my room and . . ."

"No, sweetheart, we aren't moving, don't worry," Nancy reassured her. "Your dad and I are discussing buying a place and using it to go and visit on vacations, kind of like the one we were just on, but it would be our own house. When you are all grown up, we might spend more time down there, but not until everyone is ready for that. It's a long time away."

Susie was satisfied with that answer. She ordered another Coke from the server, pulled her iPod out of her sweater and tuned out.

"What about location?" Nancy continued. "I think we should check out California. We haven't been there since our honeymoon in Palm Springs a decade ago. Why don't we go during March break? We could research places until then and check out the Palm Springs area, that whole valley area has potential. And what about Phoenix? I am sure we could find a town home in a good neighborhood and rent it out. It's worth revisiting that option as well, don't you think? No matter what or where we end up buying though, Ted, we can't treat it like a Boxing Day sale. I would rather wait and choose something that fits us, you know."

Ted laughed at the shopping analogy, especially since he has seen Nancy come home with her share of Boxing Day mistakes. But this, of course, was a house, not a sweater, and she was right. He also liked that she was now more involved, taking charge, and that they finally agreed.

Ted signaled for the bill and handed the server his credit card. A couple of minutes later, the waiter returned to tell Ted the credit card was declined.

"What?" Ted asked, shocked.

Nancy quickly pulled her card from her purse and handed it to the server. "This will work; sorry about that," she said.

She then pulled out a pen and started listing their expenses on a napkin.

"How could that happen? We have a huge credit limit," Ted asked.

"Well, we just put the new roof on that card—remember, we wanted the points from the Visa card. And don't forget that when you rent a car they put a hold on it for more than you actually plan to spend. I bet that's what happened. Plus all of this eating out, and some shopping . . ."

"Some shopping," Ted said. "How many new T-shirts did you buy Susie, and that purse you got when you went out with Sarah? How much was that?"

"Ted, don't blame this on me. We have the money, we just have to be more diligent with where it's going," Nancy said.

"We are spending a lot on looking for this US home. I guess I didn't factor that in – the price of actually finding the place," Ted said.

"Well, we have the money in our savings account to pay off the Visa card, so don't worry. I get my annual bonus next month . . . But yes, you're right, this investment will cost us money, a lot of money, up front. Let's just make sure we're more careful from now on. Let's keep good track of it all, okay?"

Susie, seeing her parents worried about money, made a suggestion: "Dad, maybe we should go back and get a credit card from those nice people with the teddy bears."

"No, Susie, that's not the answer," Ted said, patting his daughter on the head. "Nice try, though."

The server brought back the bill and Nancy's card. She signed the slip and they left the restaurant, a little embarrassed. They then hunkered down outside their departure gate and waited for their connecting flight.

HOME SWEET HOME

At 8:00 the next morning, just five hours after they finally arrived back home in Vancouver, Ted poured himself a coffee and sat down in front of his computer. He had 97 emails. One of the most recent was from Sid. Ted opened it immediately, ignoring the others. It was a list of websites related to buying property in the US and names of a few professionals that could help answer their questions. Ted hit the "print" button and then read through his other emails.

As he scrolled, Ted stopped at an email from a colleague with the subject: "BC man pepper sprayed when he asked the border guard to say 'please.'"

Ted opened the email and read it.

"Nancy!" he shouted. "Nancy! Come and listen to this."

Nancy, who was in the kitchen making coffee, shuffled towards Ted in her slippers and robe. "What is it? What's the matter?"

"Nancy, let me read you this story. You have to hear this: "A British Columbian man who wanted a US border inspector to say please got a face full of pepper spray instead. The man says he thought the guard who told him to turn off his engine Monday was rude and asked him to say please. The 54-year-old says he was stunned and blinded as he was sprayed, pulled out of the car and handcuffed. He was detained about three hours."

"Is this really true?"

"I guess so. Listen to this part: 'A US Customs and Border Protection official says it was a lawful order that travelers must obey, but the use of force is under review.' Wow, remind me not to ask those border guards anything!" Ted said.

"That's unbelievable. I wonder if he'll have any more trouble crossing the border after that," Nancy said.

She then headed back to the kitchen and pulled a coffee mug from the cupboard.

Ted followed her, holding the print out of Sid's email.

"Sid sent us a whole bunch of information that I think will really help us learn more about buying property in the US. There's a half dozen websites, and he's given us the names of some professionals who can help us out with information. He's also sent a scorecard about how to pick a good neighborhood to invest in and a list about how to find a good realtor. Want to see?"

Nancy took the paper from Ted and quickly scanned the page.

"Looks good to me. Can you forward that to my email? I'll take a look today at work. Maybe tonight we can sit down and talk about whom to contact first?"

Ted rushed back to his computer, passing Susie on the way. She walked into the kitchen, grabbed her lunch off the counter and headed out the door for her first day back to school after the Christmas holiday.

Nancy poured herself a coffee, and one for Ted, adding milk and two sugars to his cup, and set it down beside him at the computer.

Ted, still scanning the printout of Sid's email, read aloud the types of professionals on Sid's list. It included an accountant who could talk about basic information on how to buy property in the US. The accountant could also outline the different taxes to consider, from withholding tax, to capital gains if you sell the place and inheritance tax in the event one or both of the owners dies.

"That's morbid," Ted said.

"But necessary to know," added Nancy. "What else does he say?"

"He says we should talk to a mortgage broker about possibly taking money out of our home to help with the US investment."

"I'm still a bit nervous about that, but we should check it out," Nancy said. "What about a good place to find properties? Does he have anyone who can help with that?"

"It's not listed here, but I remember Sid telling me there are seminars in major Canadian cities put on by outfits that try to help people like us buy down there. We could try to find one of those and see what it's all about."

Ted reminded Nancy that he had a number for a realtor in Phoenix from the brothers he met at the basketball game there last fall.

"I have a colleague at work whose mother lives in California. I'll see if she knows any good realtors down there," Nancy said. "I think we should try to get as many references as we can, to avoid an experience like you had in Phoenix."

Nancy looked at the clock in the living room and dropped her mug on the dining room table. "I've got to go or I'll be late for work. Let's talk more about this tonight, okay?" She gave Ted a kiss on the forehead and rushed to get changed before heading out to catch her bus.

Ted stayed at his computer and bookmarked Sid's suggested websites under the heading "US Properties." He then started plowing through the long list of emails that piled up in his inbox during his week away.

TIME TO CALL IN THE EXPERTS

At 6 p.m., Ted walked in the door, soaking wet. "Wow, it's really pouring out there. Can't believe I forgot my umbrella."

"We're not in Florida anymore," Nancy shouted from the kitchen, where she was making dinner. She came out carrying a bowl of mashed potatoes and set it on the dining room table, then went back to get the chicken and salad. Susie was setting the table.

"Smells good. When will it be ready?" Ted asked.

"Two minutes. Stay off that computer and come sit. We'll talk about Sid's email after dinner. I've been looking through his information and I have some ideas," Nancy said.

As they ate, Susie talked about her day at school, including the essay she had to write on how she spent her Christmas vacation.

"Well, that will be fun," said Ted. "It was better than what you did last year, wasn't it?"

"That's for sure," Susie said, rolling her eyes. "That's when you left me with Grandma for a week while you went skiing."

"Well, we made up for it this year, didn't we?" Nancy said. Susie nodded in agreement.

"And we might have another surprise for you for March Break," Nancy added. "Your dad and I are thinking about a road trip to California and the Grand Canyon. Want to come?"

"Yes!" Susie shouted, stabbing her fork into the air and spraying mashed potatoes in several directions.

"But first you have to clear the table and let Mommy and I make plans for the trip, okay?" Ted said.

Susie cleared the table in record time and rushed off to her room to call her friend. Nancy made herself a cup of tea and sat back down with Ted. He had laid out several listings he printed out from the Internet on potential properties in the US.

"You've been busy today, I see," said Nancy.

"It's fun, isn't it? Where should we start?"

"I've already started," Nancy said. "We have an appointment Friday at lunch with an accountant. He's a friend of my boss, whose brother used him when he bought a place in Arizona."

"Nancy, when you put your mind to something . . ."

"Wait, there's more," she said. "I also called our mortgage broker about possibly taking some money out of the house to put towards the purchase."

"What did he say?" Ted asked, as Nancy consulted her notes.

"He said we should first find out how much equity we can take from our home. Then we should see how much money we can borrow from an American bank. When we find out those two sums, we should decide how much we want to borrow from each. Here's an example he gave me: If we have a property worth $500,000 and $50,000 left on our mortgage, we can access up to $350,000 as long as our income can support the debt. That's without entering into high-ratio mortgage territory, which means borrowing more than 80 per cent of our home's value. When we do that, we need to start paying insurance on the loan, which we don't want or need to do. Here's the math: If our home is worth $500,000, 80 per cent of that is $400,000, minus the $50,000 we still owe on the mortgage. That leaves us with $350,000 borrowing room. Make sense?"

Ted scratched his head. "I think so, yes, but all of that pain and suffering and chipping away at this mortgage and in one swoop we add another 15 or 20 years of payments! I think I need a drink."

Ted grabbed a beer from the fridge and sat back down at the table.

"So, that means if our limit is about $250,000 US, we have lots of borrowing ability from our home, right?" Ted continued.

"True, but we don't want to leverage that much, so we should be sure to visit a mortgage broker down south next time we're there. Also, just because we have that much room doesn't mean we want to use it."

"Right, of course," Ted said.

"Also, we can't forget the exchange rate—$250,000 American could mean $300,000 Canadian depending on where the dollar sits at the time," Nancy said.

"I think we need more beer," Ted joked.

The two then spent the rest of the evening reading articles they had collected online. Nancy also made a list of books on the subject to buy and skim through before their meeting with the accountant on Friday.

Investing vs Speculating: What Really Drives Property Values Up and Down

WAIT!!! Just because a property looks cheap, doesn't mean it is undervalued. Cheap does not mean good in real estate. As a matter of fact, it could be a major sign of trouble. In order to be a successful and sophisticated investor, not a money-blinded speculator, it is critical that you remove the emotions from the investment equation. The only way to do so is to understand what really drives the value of a real estate market, then ask the tough questions so you identify regions with a future, not just a past.

In any market conditions, in any country, there are regions that will under-perform and other regions that will out-perform. Sadly, many investors like to invest based on past performance so they're constantly chasing the market. That's called speculating—not investing. Your job is to avoid biased sales pitches and your own pre-conceived ideas, and find these hidden regions poised to out-perform. Then become a specialist and learn that area better than anyone else, know what the property market is doing on a monthly basis, what the economy is doing, what's happening in local politics and where the revitalization is going to occur. Once you become a specialist in an area, your risk is dramatically reduced, your ability to find truly undervalued properties increases and the time it takes to become successful drops significantly.

Focus on the Fundamentals, Not Emotions

To dramatically reduce your risk, ask the key questions and don't fall in love with a property. There are 12 major influences on the long-term values of property and they work in every major country in the world. Each of these affects real estate prices in both directions, and each one is an important component in finding which way real estate values will be going. The more 'yes' answers you get, the better the market will perform and the lower your risks will be. Get answers to ALL of them, for every one you skip you willfully increase your risks.

1. Is the area's average income increasing faster than provincial/state average?
2. Is the area's population growing faster than the provincial/state average?
3. Is the area creating jobs faster than the provincial/state average?
4. Does the area have more than one major employer?
5. Is the real estate booming in the surrounding region more than where you're looking?
6. Will the property value benefit from a major new development nearby?
7. Has the local and provincial/state political leadership created a "growth atmosphere?"
8. Is the region's Economic Development Office helpful and pro-active?

9. Is the neighborhood located in an area of renewal or gentrification? Or is it in a "war zone?"
10. Is there a major transportation improvement occurring nearby?
11. Is the area attractive to "Baby Boomers?"
12. Is a short-term perceived problem (negative media stories, short term layoffs) occurring that will disappear?

And most importantly of all:

Do you have someone to impeccably manage the property? Without quality management (even if it's you) no matter how good the area, the property will always under-perform and be undervalued.

Source: Excerpted from *Real Estate Investing in Canada* by Don Campbell, **www.myREINspace.com**.

How to Find a Good Real Estate Agent

A real estate agent is a very important part of your team when searching for property. He or she can save you thousands of dollars and lots of time. Good agents are worth their weight in gold. Here are 10 top considerations when looking for a good agent:

1. Trust your gut: Don't ignore your feelings when you first meet. Trust your instincts and ask yourself, "Do I really trust and like this person?"

2. **It's all about you:** Is this person focused on your needs? If your agent is taking calls continually while with you, ask yourself if he or she is really taking you seriously, and how important are you to this person?

3. **Get to know about your agent before you know him or her:** Ask the agent for referrals before you begin working together. A good agent will be happy to recommend clients, both past and present.

4. **Canuck focused:** You don't have to deal with an agent who focuses on Canadians buying south of the border. However, it can help if an agent understands how the process differs in the US.

5. **Market knowledge:** Test potential agents on how much they know the area, and how up to date they are on recent transactions. After all, they are the experts. Unfortunately, not all agents are as up to speed on their area as they should be.

6. **Presentation:** How agents present themselves is often a reflection on how they do business. For example, if they pick you up in a car that looks unkempt and has files and garbage scattered throughout, there's a higher chance that they are disorganized.

7. **Promptness:** If they arrive late all the time, it could be an indication of how seriously they take deadlines. This could make the difference in getting a deal or not.

8. **Fees:** Agents should be clear about their fees. You should also attempt to negotiate. This is not disrespectful but good business, and more importantly, will give you an insight into how they negotiate and how they will negotiate on your behalf.

9. Full-time job: It's wise to work with a full-time agent whose sole focus is real estate.

10. Does your agent own property?: If your agent rents and is pushing you to buy, ask yourself if that's the kind of person you want doing your deals. Also, if he or she owns real estate, where is it? For example, if your agent is working in Phoenix but invests in Dallas, does he or she really believe in the market? You want an agent who is focused on a particular area as opposed to an entire city or state.

Source: Philip McKernan Inc., **www.philipmckernan.com**

Accessing Equity in Your Home

Home equity is the current market value of your home, minus any outstanding debt registered against your property, such as your mortgage balance.

For instance, if you have a $50,000 mortgage and you want to borrow up to 80% on a home appraised at $500,000:

80% of the value of your home:	$400,000
Less the outstanding mortgage:	$50,000
Funds available to be borrowed:	$350,000

A high-ratio mortgage is one that needs to be insured when a down payment is less than 20% of the purchase price of a home. In Canada, three companies—CMHC, Genworth Financial and AIG—provide high-ratio mortgage insurance to home buyers who are buying their homes with less than 20% down. The insurance premium protects the lender in the event the mortgage is not repaid and the bank has to take back the property. The benefit to the borrower is that it allows them to purchase a home with less than 20% down. The insurance premium is paid by the borrower and can be added directly onto the mortgage.

Note that mortgage loan insurance is not to be confused with mortgage life insurance, which is a separate option when taking out a mortgage.

Sandbox Rules for Financing the Purchase of a US Property

As a Canadian, you can approach an American lender in the city you're choosing to buy in and ask for a loan. The rules of that bank will vary by state. Any US bank can grant a mortgage to a Canadian, but since the recent credit crisis, lending terms have tightened up. You may find that you will need to put down more money than you originally expected and the interest rate may not be as attractive as what you can get in Canada.

The simplest and least expensive way to buy real estate in the US is to access equity in your Canadian real estate and pay cash for the US purchase. This process is very simple: you will need to do an Equity Take Out (ETO) on one of your existing properties—either your principal residence or a rental property. This ETO can take the form of refinancing the property with a new first mortgage, or simply setting up a Home Equity Line of Credit

(HELOC). Ideally, you will be able to arrange a HELOC for this purpose.

There is a key difference between a HELOC and a new first mortgage. When you refinance your property and get a new first mortgage for the purpose of tapping into the equity, you will start making principal and interest payments on the entire amount of the new mortgage from day one, regardless of whether you utilize the full amount from day one.

Conversely, if you use a HELOC to refinance your home, you will be setting up a Line of Credit (LOC) that will be registered as a second mortgage on the property. The essential difference between a LOC and a mortgage is that a LOC gives you access to equity, whereas a new first mortgage actually gives you the funds. The key here is that if you have access to funds through a LOC, you will be required only to make interest-only payments and only on the amount of funds you borrow at the time you borrow them. This can be a less costly way of accessing your equity. It's also important to note that when you access equity in your line of credit on your principal residence for an investment that has the intention of making money, then the interest on the amount borrowed can be tax-deductible. (Check with your accountant before making this assumption.)

Also, remember there is no guarantee your lender will allow you to set up a LOC to access the equity in your home. You will still need to qualify based on the strength of your income, or, in the case of a rental property, the strength of your income and portfolio.

Keep in mind the impact of your decision. If you access equity in your existing properties, you will negatively impact either your personal debt service limits or your positive cash flow since you won't be able to claim revenue from a US-based investment to help offset the increase in mortgage costs. This does not mean that you shouldn't do it—just that you should do your homework and make sure the decisions you make today are congruent with your overall plan and objectives.

Some Canadian banks have increased their diligence on LOCs and are asking for details on the use of funds. Prior to 2007, you could set up a LOC with virtually any bank and there was no need to explain what you were using the funds for—after all it was your money (equity). Today, they are becoming increasingly aware and concerned about clients making poor investments and not being able to repay their LOCs. So, don't be surprised if you encounter some additional scrutiny when applying for an ETO.

Where to Start

If you're planning to buy something in the States or Mexico or wherever, I suggest you start by finding out how much equity you qualify for from your Canadian holdings. Set up new lines of credit on both your principal residence and/ or rental properties. Remember, other than legal fees and appraisals, there is no extra cost to you to establish the maximum amount of money available to you in your lines of credit. You only pay interest on the actual money you borrow, so as an investor, it will make sense for you to determine the maximum amount you can establish.

Finally, do some research in the market where you're planning to buy. Find out what financing options are open to you or available through local financial institutions.

Regardless of whether you're in Florida or Arizona, every city will have a local option, and in some cases the local option could very well be a Canadian bank.

Once you determine what the local lending option is, you can simply use your Canadian Line of Credit to top up the difference. If there is no local option, then you will need to pay cash for the entire purchase and the amount of money you can access in Canada will determine or limit how much you can buy.

Source: Peter Kinch, president of the Peter Kinch Mortgage Team (PKMT) a division of Dominion Lending Centers

NANCY'S CHECKLIST

- Build a team of professionals to help you with your real estate purchase, including:
  - ○ Accountant: For counseling and advice on tax issues related to buying, selling and renting your US property, as well as estate tax considerations.
  - ○ Financial planner: For counseling and advice on your investment goals and how the purchase fits in with your other investment objectives.
  - ○ Canadian mortgage broker or lender: For counseling and advice on options such as using equity from your current home in Canada towards a purchase of a US property.
  - ○ American mortgage broker or lender: For counseling and advice regarding financing options for your potential US property.

- ○ US real estate agent: To help you sort through listings and learn more about the neighborhoods where you're considering investing.
- ○ Lawyer: For counseling and advice on anything legal and to ensure the small print is covered. Remember the system is similar but the US is a foreign jurisdiction.
- Don't treat bank money, or equity in your home, any different than cash.

6

Of Ownership, Death and Taxes

Ted and Nancy stepped into the elevator of the bank tower in downtown Vancouver, on their way to meet the accountant.

"I can't believe we paid 20 bucks to park in that lot for two hours. There should be valet parking for that kind of money!" Ted complained as the elevator shot up to the 18th floor.

"You could have at least worn a dress shirt to this meeting, you know," Nancy said.

"What? It's Friday and I'm off for the rest of the day. Do I have to look good for the accountant?" Ted said in defense of his gray T-shirt and blue jeans. "Besides, maybe if I *look* poor we'll get some special advice on how to save money. They'll know we're not rich."

"It doesn't work that way, Ted," Nancy said, exasperated, but she had had that conversation before, many times, and decided not to press the point any further.

She reached into her handbag and pulled out a digital tape recorder. She noticed Ted's quizzical look.

"I bought this to tape the meeting, so that we can listen to the information again later. We can then download the audio onto the computer."

Ted was constantly amazed at how organized his wife was. He didn't even bring a pen to the meeting. The elevator opened to the 18th floor and the two stepped out. Nancy checked the directory on the wall for the accountant's suite number.

"Here it is, suite 1800. This way," Nancy said.

The office was a modest size, filled with cubicles and a slim view of BC's North Shore mountains hidden mostly by adjacent office towers. Nancy checked in with the receptionist and they took a seat in the waiting area. Ted flipped through a dated copy of *Maclean's* and was about to pick up a pamphlet on tax-saving tips when the accountant came to greet them.

"I'm Nick, nice to meet you," said the accountant, who looked fresh out of college, dressed neatly in a blue shirt and tie, black pinstriped slacks and shiny black shoes. He led Ted and Nancy down the hall to his office. As they followed, Ted turned to Nancy and whispered, "This is the guy your co-worker recommended? Is it their son? He's a kid."

"Shhh. They said he's very good and I have no reason to believe otherwise."

Nick stopped, turned and smiled and invited them to take a seat in his small office.

"When I graduate they'll give me a bigger office," Nick said, then sat down.

Ted laughed, while Nancy blushed in embarrassment.

"Don't worry; I get those kinds of comments all the time. I've actually been doing this for 10 years now. I just look young for my age, which is 34. I can answer all of your questions and, if I can't, I will definitely find someone here who can."

"I'm sorry about that, Nick," said Nancy.

"Don't be," Nick said. "Now how can I help you? I believe Nancy said the two of you were interested in buying property in the US? Is that correct?"

Nancy and Ted nodded in unison.

"First, let me start by explaining my fee structure. The initial half hour consultation we're doing now is free. My rate thereafter is $295 an hour plus disbursements," Nick said. "Any questions?"

"Nope," Ted said. He then started to explain their situation.

"We nearly bought something in Phoenix last fall, but I think it was fate that it didn't work out. We've looked around a bit, and we've got a friend who's in the game down in Florida, the real estate game—owns a few properties—and we got some advice from him. Mostly he pushed us to have a plan and a good reason to buy . . ."

Nancy cut him off. "We've done some research, but we want to make sure we have all the facts, on taxes and things, before we start looking seriously."

Nick listened as Nancy explained some of the considerations they'd heard about, including restrictions on how long you can stay in the US and withholding tax, as well as the different state taxes and the estate tax should one of them die while owning a property in the United States.

"Sounds like you have been doing some homework," Nick said. "That's good."

He then pulled a file from the top of a stack of papers and opened it.

"There are various financial considerations when buying a property in the US. What I've done here is pull some documents our firm prepares for our clients outlining the basic information potential US property buyers should know."

Nick handed a binder to Ted and Nancy.

"That's a lot of reading," Ted said, flipping through the pages.

"It's the basic information," Nick said. "I thought it would be best to give you this information, and if you have any specific questions, either today or at another time, you can always ask me."

Nick also handed each of them a copy of his business card.

"Now, if you don't mind, I'd like to go through this document with you and just point out some of the main considerations," Nick said.

He explained that there are many factors to think about, on both sides of the border. "Knowing all the different variables before you buy can save you a lot of hassle, and a lot of money, down the road."

He said Canadians must advise the Canada Revenue Agency if they buy property in the US and collect rental income from it, and when they sell it.

"We have to tell the taxman everything, don't we?" Ted commented. "I'm afraid so," said Nick. "It's also your responsibility, as a US property owner, to know all of the rules. The Internal Revenue Service, or IRS, which is the US taxman, is pretty tough. Ignorance won't help get you off the hook if you owe them money. But that's why you are here, right? So let's get started."

Nancy pulled out her digital recorder and asked Nick if it was okay for her to tape the conversation.

"Absolutely, no problem," said Nick. "I wish more of my clients did that."

The first thing Nick asked is if they owned their own home in Canada. They nodded.

"That's good. That means you already know a lot about buying property," Nick said. "Buying property in the US is not any more complex than the process here in Canada; you just need to know and follow all of the income tax rules. It's the legal and tax difference that making buying a house down south seem difficult. But my job is to make it easy for you to understand. Also, remember that this is a general overview and that there will be specific, more detailed considerations depending on your individual circumstances, as well as where you buy in the US."

"We understand," said Nancy, who was already taking notes.

Nick then asked Ted and Nancy to turn to the first page of the papers he gave them.

"Okay," Nick began, "I'd like to start with what I think is one of the most common oversights Canadians have when investing in US property, and that is a lack of thinking through the rationale for buying a property there. There's a lot of debate in our profession over the best way to offer counsel on this decision, but I think it's really up to the buyers to decide what's best for them with respect to their personal circumstances."

Nick said there are three main types of ownership: personal, joint or through a corporation or trust. "Personal ownership is the simplest way to hold US property," Nick said. "Joint ownership, where the property is in both your names, is also very common for married couples. You can also set up a corporation or trust, which can offer the most asset protection, but that also depends on your circumstances. As I said, there is no one-fits-all structure, so it's best to find the one that works for you and your circumstances. This is important not just for estate-tax purposes, but because there are tax consequences to trying to change your options after you purchase the property."

Nick then pointed to an article about types of ownership and estate tax, and recommended they read it when they had some spare time after the meeting.

Types of Ownership and Estate Tax

Without proper planning in place, a Canadian's estate may be required to pay US estate tax on the value of the US home. Rates start at 18% and rise quickly to 45% for properties worth more than US$1.5 million. The Canada-US Tax Treaty, however, provides some relief for Canadians.

How the Exemptions Work

For US citizens, the first US$3.5 million in assets is exempt from the US estate tax. The Treaty entitles Canadians to a percentage of that exemption, which is the proportion of value of the individual's US assets to worldwide assets. For example, if US property represents 20% of worldwide assets, the deceased will be entitled to an exemption of US$700,000 (20% of 3.5 million).

The Treaty provides additional relief if the US property of the deceased passes to a Canadian spouse. In general, this provision will double the exemption (calculated above) if all of the assets pass to the surviving spouse.

The US annual exemption increased to US$3.5 million in 2009. However, unless new legislation is enacted, in 2011 the exemption will decrease to its earlier level of to US$1 million and the 45% top rate reverts to 55%. Most practitioners believe the 2009 rates will be extended. While nothing is certain, it seems prudent to plan on the assumption that the US estate tax will be around in some form beyond 2009.

Personal Ownership

Personal ownership may be the simplest way to hold property if the US estate tax liability can be managed or eliminated. The best approach for married individuals may be to put ownership in the hands of the spouse with the lower net worth. However, one must consider the Canadian income tax attribution rules if the spouse doesn't have his or her own source of funds to complete the purchase. Under these rules, for Canadian tax purposes the property could be considered to belong to the other spouse.

If the home is owned personally, individual wills should be reviewed. It may be possible to eliminate US estate tax if the US property passes to a properly structured spousal trust on death.

Personal Ownership in Joint Tenancy

Joint tenancy is a common form of ownership for Canadians. However, joint tenancy for a US property is generally not a recommended form of ownership for Canadian spouses. For US estate tax purposes, the entire value of the property is included in the US estate of the first spouse to die, unless the executor can prove that the surviving spouse contributed funds towards the purchase of the property. In addition, joint tenancy does not allow for any will planning to take place because the property will pass automatically to the surviving spouse. Owning the property as tenants-in-common may be an effective alternative because it would allow each spouse to undertake will planning to protect his or her half interest.

A Canadian Trust

If the US estate tax cannot be dealt with through personal ownership and the provisions of a will, consider establishing a Canadian discretionary family trust to hold the ownership of the property. The two key benefits are that:

- US estate tax may be avoided on the death of both parties, and
- If the property is sold, any increase in the value will be subject to the same capital gains rates as if the property were owned personally.

Trust ownership generally appeals to Canadians when property values exceed US$1 million and do not constitute a significant portion of the individual's net worth. This is because the individual must be willing to give up control over the property to his or her spouse and children. In addition, because of Canada's 21-year rule, the trust likely will distribute the property to the capital beneficiaries before its 21st anniversary and avoid a deemed realization of accrued gains. Therefore, the trust structure may not appeal to younger families.

Other Options

If personal or trust ownership doesn't fit the circumstances, other options should be considered, including:

- ownership through a Canadian corporation
- ownership through a Canadian partnership
- donation of the property to a US-registered charity

In some cases, if the US estate tax exposure cannot be fully eliminated, it might be best to obtain additional life insurance that can adequately cover a tax bill. This could be the simplest solution for younger purchasers, who have access to low-cost insurance.

It is wise to consider all ownership options before entering into a purchase agreement. Many planning techniques cannot be used after the US property is purchased because of the US gift and income-tax consequences associated with the transfer of US real estate.

Source: **PricewaterhouseCoopers**.

Nick also pointed out that if Nancy and Ted bought a property and it was in both of their names, they must each file a federal and state tax return where required. "Failure to do so can carry pretty big financial penalties. Also, you don't want to be in the IRS's bad books," Nick said.

"No, our own taxman is frightening enough," said Ted. "I've got enough trouble getting one set of tax returns done. Are you saying we have to file a US tax return as well?"

Nick smiled. "Any questions?"

"Can you tell us more about these rules, about how long we could actually spend at the place if we bought it? We've heard a bit about this, but would like to get something more official from you," Nancy asked.

Nick nodded and asked them to turn to the second page of the materials he gave them.

"In the US, you're either a 'resident alien' or a 'non-resident alien,' " said Nick.

"So we're aliens no matter what," Ted joked.

"That's right, Ted," Nick replied. "It's all about whether you are required to pay tax on your income to the US government. As a 'resident alien' you pay income tax on worldwide income. It's as though you're living in the US. You also get to make the same deductions and personal exemptions. A 'non-resident alien' pays tax on income only earned in the US, subject to limited deductions and exemptions. The threshold is how long you reside in the US. If it's less than 183 days, you are a non-resident alien. That's about half of 365 days, or six months a year. But the official way to figure that out is in what the US government calls the 'substantial presence test.' Turn to the information we've put together from both the IRS and CRA web sites."

Ted and Nancy turned to the documents under the heading "Substantial Presence Test Requirements."

The Substantial Presence Test Requirements

You will be considered a US resident for tax purposes if you meet the substantial presence test for the calendar year. To meet this test, you must be physically present in the United States on at least:

1. 31 days during the current year, and
2. 183 days during the 3-year period that includes the current year and the 2 years immediately before that, counting:
   - All the days you were present in the current year, and
   - 1/3 of the days you were present in the first year before the current year, and
   - 1/6 of the days you were present in the second year before the current year.

For instance, to determine whether you meet the substantial presence test for 2008, calculate the number of days you were present in the US during 2008, 2007 and 2006. The days do not have to be consecutive, and you

---

are treated as being present in the US on any day you were there for part or all of the day. Each day:

- in 2008 counts as a full day;
- in 2007 counts as one-third of a day; and
- in 2006 counts as one-sixth of a day.

If your total is at least 183 days, you have met the substantial presence test and you are considered a resident alien for 2008. If your total is less than 183 days, you are considered a non-resident alien for 2008.

Example:

Florence and Henry are residents of Canada and own a trailer home in Florida, where they spend each winter. Although they have no US source income, they need to determine their US residency status. To do this, they have to determine how many days they were in the US during 2008, 2007 and 2006.

During 2008, they were in the US from January 1 to April 10, and from November 13 to December 31 (150 days). During 2007, they were in the US from January 1 to March 31, and from November 14 to December 31 (138 days). During 2006, they were in the US from January 1 to April 5, and from November 1 to December 31 (156 days).

Each day they were in the US during 2008 counts as a full day (150). Each day they were in the US during 2007 counts as one-third of a day (138 multiplied by one-third = 46). Each day they were in the US during 2006 counts as one-sixth of a day (156 multiplied by one-sixth = 26).

They add the subtotals: 150 + 46 + 26 = 222. Since this total is at least 183 days during the 3-year period, they meet the substantial presence test and are considered resident aliens by the US for 2008.

Sources: Internal Revenue Service/Canada Revenue Agency websites.

"I like that Florence and Henry example," Nancy said. "That helps put it into perspective."

"Sounds like a lot of legalese to me," said Ted.

"It's very complicated," Nick replied. "Now, just to further complicate things, I need to tell you about the exceptions to the substantial presence test. It's also explained on those sheets I gave you, but basically if you have what's called a 'closer connection' to the US or you have a special job that requires you to be down there for long periods of time, such as a government employee or a teacher with a special visa, then you're considered an exception. There's also Treaty tie-breaker provisions. I don't think any of these apply to the two of you, from what I know so far, but it's there for you to examine."

Exceptions to the Substantial Presence Test

For Canadians snared by the substantial presence test, all is not lost. There are three exceptions to the test, which allow a Canadian to still be taxed as a non-resident: the closer-connection-to-a-foreign-country exception, the exempt individual exception and the treaty tiebreaker provisions.

Exception 1: Closer Connection

An individual who, despite meeting the substantial presence test, maintains a closer connection to a foreign country will not be treated as meeting the test for the current year if:

- The individual is present in the US fewer than 183 days during the current year;
- The individual maintains a tax home (e.g., a main place of business or employment; or, if an individual has no such place, then the place where he/she regularly lives) in a foreign country during the current year; and
- The individual has a closer connection during the current year to a single foreign country in which he/she maintains a tax home than to the US.

An individual may generally establish that his/her tax home is in a foreign country by showing that his/her principal place of business or employment and/or abode are located in such foreign country. The tax home must be in existence for the entire taxable year and must be in the foreign country to which the individual claims a closer connection. Thus, the closer-connection exception generally will not apply to the year an individual moves to the US.

The determination of whether an individual has a closer connection to such foreign country will generally be made by weighing the individual's contacts with the US against those with the foreign country. Such contacts include the location of one's:

1. regular or principal permanent home
2. family
3. automobiles
4. personal belongings
5. social, cultural, religious and political organizations
6. banks with which an individual conducts routine personal banking activities
7. registration to vote
8. investments

Both the tax-home and closer-connection determinations are factual in nature and therefore subject to some degree of uncertainty. Therefore, a Canadian should generally rely on the closer-connection-to-a-foreign-country exception only as a last resort. Furthermore, this exception will not apply for any year during which the individual has an application pending for adjustment to permanent resident status or has taken other affirmative steps to apply for status as a lawful permanent resident of the US.

In order to qualify for the closer connection exception to the substantial presence test, an individual must file a form with the IRS.

Exception 2: Exempt Individual

Under the exempt-individual exception, an individual generally will not be treated as being present in the US on any day in which he/she is temporarily present in the US as a foreign government-related individual, a teacher or trainee who holds a J visa, a student holding either an F, J or M visa, or a professional athlete temporarily in the US to compete in a charitable sports event.

Exempt individuals are required to file a form with the IRS stating why they are exempt from US taxation.

Exception 3: Treaty Tie-Breaker Provisions

It is possible that a Canadian will be considered to be a resident of both Canada and the US pursuant to the tax laws in each country. The Canada-United State Income Tax Convention (the Treaty) provides relief from being considered a resident of both locations as follows:

1. An individual shall be deemed to be a resident solely of the country in which he/she has a permanent home available;
2. If a permanent home is available in both countries, or if a permanent home is not available in either country, the individual will be deemed to be a resident solely in the country with which his/her personal and economic relations are the closer (center of vital interests).
3. If the center of vital interests cannot be determined, he/she will be deemed to be a resident of the country in which he/she has a habitual abode;
4. If a habitual abode is available in both countries or in neither country, he/she will be deemed to be a resident of the country of which he/she is a citizen;
5. If he/she is a citizen of both countries, or of neither, the competent authorities of the countries will settle the question by mutual agreement.

Although an individual who holds a US permanent resident visa may claim to be a non-resident of the US pursuant to the Treaty, it is advisable that the individual consult with his/her immigration attorney before claiming non-resident status. The US Income Tax Regulations provide that claiming non-resident status may affect the determination by the Immigration and Naturalization Service as to whether the individual qualifies to maintain a residency permit.

A tax return must be filed in a timely fashion to claim the Treaty tie-breaker provisions. Failure to file within the time limits may result in significant penalties.

Source: KPMG.

Ted scratched his head. "That's a bit confusing, but I guess we aren't planning on spending that much time down there for at least another 10 or 15 years, so we can worry about it later."

"It's just good to know," Nancy said. "We are kind of hoping to buy a place and rent it out maybe for the first few years. But we haven't figured out exact details yet."

Nick rocked back and forth in his chair, listening as Nancy described their goals, short and long term.

"Well, let's talk a bit about what happens when you rent out a property. I can show you how the taxation works. Of course, you have to claim income in both the US and Canada, but it's not as bad as it sounds at first."

"Any tax sounds bad, but it's a necessary evil I guess, isn't it?" asked Ted.

"Unfortunately, Ted, that's true," said Nick. "I have attached another article on the taxation of rental property to these handouts, but generally speaking, rental income on your US real estate must be reported on both of your US and

Canadian federal tax returns. Also, there are some US states that also require you to pay tax on rental income, such as Arizona and California, but not Florida or Texas, for example. You also file a special form that allows you to claim a tax credit to avoid double taxation in the US and Canada. There are also deductions for depreciation and any allowable expense on income properties. I encourage you to read the article, it explains it in detail."

Tax Implications of Renting US Property

Many Canadians own US recreational property near border states. Retired Canadians who are seasonal residents of the US, or "Snowbirds," frequently own property in the US.

If either of the above situations applies to you, you may be renting out your US property on a part-time or full-time basis when you are not using it. If so, you are considered a "non-resident alien" by the IRS (the US Internal Revenue Service) and you are subject to US income tax on the rental income.

Tax on Gross Rental Income

The rent you receive is subject to a 30% withholding tax, which your tenant or property management agent is required to deduct and remit to the IRS. It doesn't matter if the tenants are Canadians or other non-residents of the US, or if it was paid to you while you were in Canada. The Canada-US tax treaty allows the US to tax income from real estate with no reduction in the general withholding rate. As rental income is not considered to be effectively connected, it is subject to a flat 30% tax on gross income, with no expenses or deductions allowed. The 30% withholding tax would therefore equal the flat tax rate.

Tax on Net Rental Income

Since a tax rate of 30% of gross income is high, you may prefer to elect to pay tax on net income, after all deductible expenses. This would result in reduced tax payable and perhaps none at all. The Internal Revenue Code permits this option, if you choose to permanently treat rental income as income that is effectively connected with the conduct of a US trade or business. You would then be able to claim expenses related to owning and operating a rental property during the rental period, such as mortgage interest, property tax, utilities, insurance and maintenance.

You can also deduct an amount for depreciation on the building. However, the IRS only permits individuals (rather than corporations) to deduct the mortgage or loan interest relating to the rental property if the debt is secured by the rental property or other business property. If you borrow the funds in Canada, secured by your Canadian assets, you would not technically be able to deduct that interest on your US tax return. Obtain strategic tax planning advice on this issue.

Once you have made the election, it is valid for all subsequent years, unless approval to revoke it is requested and received from the IRS. However, you do need to file an annual return.

If you want to be exempt from the non-resident withholding tax and are making that election, you have to give your tenant or property management agent a Form 4224,

Exemption from Withholding Tax on Income Effectively Connected with the Conduct of a Trade or Business in the US. Contact the IRS for further information.

When you file your annual return, show the income and expenses, as well as the tax withheld. If you end up with a loss after deducting expenses from income, you are entitled to a refund of the taxes withheld. The due date of your return is June 15th of the following year.

It is important to file on a timely basis. If you fail to file on the due date, you have 16 months thereafter to do so. If you don't do so, you will be subject to tax on the gross income basis for that year, that is, 30% of gross rents with no deduction for any expenses incurred, even if you made the net income election in a previous year. This is an important caution to keep in mind. Many people don't arrange to have tax withheld at source, or file any US tax forms, on the premise that their expenses exceed the rental income and the net income election is always available.

Filing Requirements

You are required to report the gain or loss on sale by filing Form 1040 NR, US Non-Resident Alien Income Tax Return. You would have to pay US federal tax on any gain (capital gain), and if you own the real estate jointly with another person, such as your spouse, each of you have to file the above form. For more information, contact the IRS.

In addition, you would have to report any capital gain on the sale of your US property in your next annual personal tax return filing with Revenue Canada. Remember, you have to report your worldwide income and gains and

> pay tax on 75% of any capital gain, converted to the equivalent in Canadian dollars, at the time of sale.
>
> Since tax laws, regulations and filing forms can change at any time, make sure you speak to a professional accountant who is skilled in US tax matters.
>
> Source: **www.snowbird.ca**, Douglas Gray, author of *Canadian Snowbird Guide*.

Nick also talked about some of the other forms they would have to file to the IRS, and the need for an "Individual Taxpayer Identification Number."

"If you are a non-resident alien who has to file a US tax return, you have to have a taxpayer identification number, or ITIN," Nick says. "You just need to apply for one; it's like a Social Security Number. If you were ever issued one of those, use it, but don't use your Canadian social insurance number. Also, having an ITIN has no impact on being allowed to live or work in the US."

Ted and Nancy were listening to Nick, like good students, as the digital recorder continued taping.

"Have I thoroughly confused you yet?" Nick asked. They appeared a bit perplexed.

"Let's keep going," Nancy said. "I think I've got most of it so far. Let's talk about what happens when we sell a property."

Nick explained that if they sold their US property, they would have to file a US income tax return. "It doesn't matter if you made a gain or loss on the sale," Nick said. "You can claim a foreign tax credit that can be used to reduce the Canadian tax on the sale, but there are a lot of conditions tied to this."

Nick referred them to more details on selling your property on another page in the materials he gave them.

Selling Your Property

If a Canadian sells real estate located in the US, a withholding tax of 10% of the gross sales price is normally payable under FIRPTA (the Foreign Investment in Real Property Tax Act of 1980). The tax withheld can be offset against the US income tax payable on any gain realized on the sale, and refunded if it exceeds the tax liability. The 10% withholding requirement on the gross sales price applies regardless of the seller's adjusted basis in the property.

There are two exceptions to FIRPTA's 10% withholding requirement, which may reduce or eliminate the requirement.

Exception 1: Sales Price Less Than US$300,000

First, withholding under FIRPTA will not apply if the property is sold for less than US$300,000, and the purchaser intends to use it as a principal residence. The buyer need not be a US resident. For this exception to apply, the purchaser must have definite plans to reside at the property for at least half of the time that the property is in use during each of the two years following the sale. However, the gain on the sale will still be taxable in the US, and a US tax return must therefore be filed. Thus, if a Canadian is selling a Florida condo or any other US real estate, for less than US$300,000 to a buyer who intends to occupy it as a principal residence, the seller will receive the full purchase price rather than having 10% withheld by the buyer and remitted to the IRS.

Exception 2: Withholding Certificate

The second exception allows for reduced, or eliminated withholding, where the Canadian obtains a withholding certificate from the IRS on the basis that the expected US tax liability will be less than 10% of the sales price. The certificate will indicate what amount of tax should be withheld by the purchaser rather than the full 10%. A withholding certificate issued after the transfer of the property may allow the seller to receive an early refund.

Filing Requirements

For income-tax purposes, a Canadian must file a US tax return and report the gain on the sale of US real estate. A credit may then claimed for the FIRPTA tax withheld.

If an individual owned the property and has been resident in Canada since before September 27, 1980 he/she can likely take advantage of the Canada-US tax treaty to reduce the gain. In such a case, only the gain accruing since January 1, 1985 will be taxed. This transitional rule does not apply to business properties that are part of a permanent establishment in the US.

To claim the benefit under the treaty, a Canadian will need to make the claim on a US tax return and include a statement containing certain specific information about the transaction.

US tax on the sale of US property will generate a foreign tax credit that can be used to reduce the Canadian tax on the sale. However, if the amount of the gain taxed

in Canada was reduced due to the capital gains exemption or the principal residence exemption, the foreign tax
credit available may be limited.

Source: KPMG.

Ted read through the tax information briefly, and then
turned over the page. "Well, I think I've had enough learning for one day."

Nancy was still reading, and Nick waited for her to stop
before continuing. After a couple minutes she looked up from
the page.

"That's a lot of detail. I don't think I'll try to memorize
that today, but it's all very good to know. Thanks, Nick. What
else should we be asking you?"

"Well, there's definitely more, but this should be
enough to get you started, unless you have any more specific
questions?"

"Not me," Ted said.

"Not today," said Nancy.

"Again, it's a lot to absorb, and I encourage you to take this
material home and read through it, and feel free to call or come
back any time with more questions," Nick said in closing.

Nancy turned off the recorder and put it back into her
purse. "That was very helpful Nick. Thank you. We have a
lot to study."

"It's a big decision," Nick said, "but a lot of people are
doing it and with prices down there so inexpensive, and
so many homes to choose from, if you can do it, why not?
It's at least worth looking into. As long as you have the

right professionals to help you through it, it can be very rewarding."

Ted and Nancy stood up to leave and shook hands with Nick.

"You've been very helpful, thanks a lot," said Ted. "And now I've got lots of stuff to read in case I have trouble falling asleep."

"Ted!" Nancy said, trying to quiet her always-chatty husband.

"Thank you, Nick. I appreciate how you've laid this out for us in a way that helps us make our decision," Nancy said.

Nick escorted them to the office foyer. As they waited for the elevator, Ted turned to Nancy, "That wasn't as bad as I thought. He knows his stuff."

"Told you so," Nancy said.

The elevator doors opened and they stepped in and rode down to the parking garage below.

NANCY'S NOTES

- Consult a lawyer or accountant with experience in the area of Canadians buying US property in the US. This includes someone who is up to date on any new changes to the laws or tax rules.
- Understand the "Substantial Presence Test" and how it could impact your investment decision, as well as the exceptions to the rules.
- Consider the different buying options, from personal or joint ownership to a trust structure.
- If you are a non-resident alien who has to file a US tax return, you must have a taxpayer identification number, or ITIN.

- Understand the tax implications, in the US and Canada, of renting your US property.
- Understand the tax implications, in both the US and Canada, of selling your US property.
- Check the IRS website for more detailed information on Canadians buying US property.
- NEVER fill out any government forms relating to US real estate or taxes without getting advice from your accountant as this may result in unnecessary taxes down the road.

Tax Strategies for Canadian Investment in U.S. Real Estate by Tom Wheelwright

While it's important to understand the tax rules for investing in U.S. real estate, it's even more important to develop a strategy that minimizes your taxes on your U.S. investment income. A tax strategy is simply a comprehensive plan to reduce or eliminate the taxes on your U.S. property investments.

There are two primary principles we recommend for Canadians investing in the U.S. The first is to avoid personal identification by the IRS. This means, don't get a U.S. taxpayer identification number or social security number if you can help it. Instead, set up a corporation in the U.S. to do your investing. The IRS has very long arms and once you get in the IRS system, you will have a difficult time getting out.

Second, set up your investments so you only pay one tax, i.e., either the U.S. tax or the Canadian tax, but not both. You will be taxed in Canada on the income you earn in the U.S. You will also be taxed in the U.S. The key, then, is the foreign tax credit you take in Canada for income earned in the U.S. The secret to ensuring you receive this credit is to make sure that the "taxpayer" (i.e., entity) in Canada is the same taxpayer as the one paying the tax in the U.S. So, if you are paying taxes in the U.S. through a corporation, you want to make sure that corporation is the entity that pays tax in both the U.S. and Canada. There are some entities, notably limited liability companies that are taxed differently in the U.S. and in Canada. As a result, you could end up paying tax in the U.S. and paying tax in Canada as well.

The other key, of course, to minimizing your tax liability is to understand the U.S. and the Canadian tax rules for real estate. Both countries allow a deduction for depreciation, only at different rates. And both countries allow a cost segregation analysis to speed up the depreciation. Depreciation is a non-cash deduction the government gives you for wear and tear on the property. Different types of property (e.g., building and contents) are depreciated at different rates. A cost segregation works to shift some of the cost of the property from the building to the faster-depreciated contents. You will need a qualified cost segregation expert (either accountant or engineer or both) to perform the cost segregation. On commercial properties, cost segregations can result in hundreds of thousands of dollars in tax savings.

There are other rules that you also need to know in the U.S., such as the passive loss rules, the 1031/like-kind exchange rules and the general rules for business and investment deductions and taxation. So, our final recommendation is to hire both a qualified Chartered Accountant in Canada who understands real estate and cross-border issues and a qualified Certified Public Accountant in the U.S. who specializes in these issues.

The good news is that with proper planning, a good tax strategy and the right advisors, you can seriously reduce and in some cases even eliminate the tax on real estate investment income.

Source: Tom Wheelwright, CPA, founder and CEO of ProVision PLC, **www.ProVisionWealth.com**.

LINKS FOR IRS ARTICLES, FORMS AND PUBLICATIONS

http://www.irs.gov/formspubs/index.html

IRS Form 8840 – Closer Connection Exception Statement for Aliens
www.irs/gov/pub/irs-pdf/f8840.pdf

IRS Form 8288 – US Withholding Tax Return for Disposition by Foreign Persons of US Real Property Interests
www.irs/gov/pub/irs-pdf/f8288.pdf

IRS Form W7 – Application for IRS Individual Tax Identification Number
www.irs/gov/pub/irs-pdf/fw7.pdf

IRS Form 1040NR – US Non-resident Alien Income Tax
Return Instructions
www.irs/gov/pub/irs-pdf/f1040nr.pdf

IRS Form Schedule D – Capital Gains and Losses
www.irs/gov/pub/irs-pdf/f1040sd.pdf

IRS Form Schedule E – Supplemental Income and Losses
www.irs/gov/pub/irs-pdf/f1040se.pdf

7

Of a California Lifestyle and a Nevada Auction

The airplane touched down in Palm Springs, marking the official start of March Break for Susie and another vacation and house hunting expedition for Ted and Nancy. The three collected their baggage from among the dozens of golf bags landing on the carousel and headed towards the rental car booth, where Ted had reserved an SUV.

"This will be a lot of fun. I bet there's not a lot of kids at school who get to spend March Break in California, Arizona and Las Vegas," Ted said as he put his arm around Susie.

"I can't believe how many cool places I've got to visit so far this year. You guys should really take your time before you buy a house," Susie said. "Maybe we should look in Europe too. How about Paris!"

"Yeah, right," said Nancy. "Tell you what, you keep taking those French classes and then you can teach your father and me how to speak French and then maybe—I am saying maybe for a reason—we can visit Paris some day."

Susie rolled her eyes as her parents laughed.

"I will say that I do like having the flexibility, Ted, to go to other places like Paris in the future," Nancy said.

"Aha! There's the car," said Ted, pointing to a black SUV and trying to change the subject.

"Wow," Nancy said. "We're traveling in style, aren't we?"

"This is California. All the movie stars drive these," Ted said.

"Are we going to see movie stars?" Susie asked, not missing a beat.

"Maybe, but probably not," Nancy replied.

"I think a lot of movie stars live in Palm Springs," Ted said.

"That might be true, but they don't hang out in the place tourists like us do," Nancy replied.

"We'll see," said Ted. "Care to place a bet on that? I bet you that on this trip we will see somebody famous. I'll bet you one month of taking out the recycling and garbage. If I'm right, and we see someone famous, you do it for a month, and if I'm wrong, I'll do it."

"You're on," Nancy said.

"You guys are silly," Susie said, as she buckled her seatbelt in the back seat.

Nancy took the passenger seat and Ted loaded their luggage in the back before jumping behind the wheel.

"Are we ready?" he said, putting the key in the ignition.

"Ready!" Nancy and Susie said in unison.

"Where to first?" Ted asked.

"We have to meet Paul, the real estate agent, in about an hour and a half," said Nancy. "How about we go get some lunch? We can check into the hotel later this afternoon."

"I'm hungry," Susie said.

"Me too," Ted said. "Although it seems like we just ate breakfast, doesn't it?"

"It's really been only three hours since we left Vancouver, but let's get something to eat. I need coffee," said Nancy. Ted drove down the highway, which was lined with palm trees and a mix of quaint rancher-style homes and complexes backing onto golf courses.

As they drove, Nancy reached into her backpack on the floor in front of her and pulled out a file folder. It contained print-outs of property listings for Palm Springs that they found on the Internet, as well as a few by Paul, the agent they found in the area on a recommendation from a friend of Nancy's at work.

"We're going to do more than just look at houses, right Mum?" Susie said, as she watched Nancy flip through a stack of listings.

"Yes, Susie. But remember the deal. Part of this trip is for Mum and Dad to find a house to invest in, and the other part of the trip is the fun Susie stuff, right?" Nancy said.

Susie rolled her eyes again. "Yes, Mum."

After a quick lunch at a local sandwich shop, they pulled into the parking lot of a realty firm where Paul was expecting them. It was in a strip mall beside a bank and a coffee shop in a charming part of the city surrounded by palm trees.

"This is a lovely city," Nancy said as they looked for a parking spot. "I have fond memories of our honeymoon here. But it's changed so much, hasn't it, Ted?"

"It has, but I bet the golfing is still world class. Are you sure we don't have time for a round of golf?" Ted asked.

"Let's see how it goes," Nancy said. "I still can't believe we played as much golf as we did when we were here last time. Some honeymoon!"

"That's back when you would have done anything I wanted to. Things sure have changed haven't they?" Ted said with a grin.

"Very funny, Ted. You should be thankful I went along with you back then. You were a terrible golfer!" Nancy shot back. "Oh, there's a good parking space there. Park there!"

Ted pulled into the space and the three hopped out of the car and then into the agent's office a few steps away.

"We're looking for Paul," Ted said to the receptionist.

Before she could call him to the front, a 40-something man in dark jeans, a blue dress shirt and slicked-back hair came down the hall holding his hand out ready to grab Ted's.

"You must be Ted; I'm Paul," said the agent. He then introduced himself to Nancy and Susie.

"How was your flight?" Paul asked.

"Great. Quick," Ted said.

"We're looking forward to seeing some properties you've sent to us on the Internet," added Nancy.

"Well, shall we get started then?" Paul asked.

They followed Paul to his Ford SUV in the parking lot.

"Have you ever been here before?" Paul asked. "To Palm Springs, I mean?"

Nancy explained that they had honeymooned in Palm Springs a decade ago, but not since.

"That's wonderful. So it's like a second honeymoon in a sense?" Paul asked.

"That depends on if I get lucky or not," said Ted, sitting in the passenger seat.

"Ted!" Nancy shouted, and punched him in the arm. "Stop that!"

Paul laughed and Nancy's face turned beet red. Susie asked what was so funny.

"Nothing, Susie. Your father is just using his bad sense of humor right now," Nancy said.

Susie shrugged and continued playing with the different buttons on the door beside her.

Paul quickly changed the subject to a bit of the history of Palm Springs.

"Are you a golfer, Ted?" Paul asked.

Ted nodded.

"Then I bet you knew this is one of the top three golf destinations in the world?"

"I think I read that somewhere, yes. Play much?" Ted asked Paul.

"Not as much as I would like to, but I try to get out once a week," Paul said.

"Once a week is like a dream for me," Ted replied.

Paul described how many golf courses in the area are closed for about three weeks a year in the early fall, for reseeding. "But that's just to make sure folks like you and I can golf here all winter long, to get away from the snow."

Paul also explained some of the Hollywood history of the place, and how a lot of stars came to the area to get away from Hollywood.

"Suzanne Somers actually lives here, as does Greg Norman, and Will Smith just bought here not too long ago as well," said Paul.

"Are we going to see movie stars?" asked Susie. "My Mom and Dad have a bet if we'll see any of them."

Paul smiled. "Is that right? What's the bet?"

"Taking out the garbage for a month," said Ted. "Hey, Paul, if you drive us by Suzanne Somers' home, I'll give you a big tip."

"That's cheating," said Nancy from the back seat, still fuming from the earlier comment.

After a few seconds, she cracked a smile and everyone laughed.

Paul then pulled into a newer neighborhood where he said most of the homes for sale were foreclosed.

"I'm sure you know all about how that happened," Paul said. "A lot of these buyers either got sucked in by the subprime loans, or they lost their jobs in the recession. It's a terrible thing, but if you've a buyer, it can be a great opportunity. Nancy, based on our conversation last week, the first home I want to show you is down this street here."

Paul turned right down a wide street lined with brand-new homes, some that were well kept, and others that, despite being brand new, had broken windows, brown grass and dead trees out front.

"This home I'm about to show you is fine in the inside, but the outside needs a bit of landscaping work," Paul warned.

"I'm sure you know all about these REO—or 'Real Estate Owned' homes. They are owned by the bank, but just to be clear they are not the same as the property up for foreclosure auction."

"Can you explain what you mean by that?" Nancy asked.

"Sure," Paul said. "First, foreclosed homes go to auction. When they can't be sold they revert to the lender, and are commonly referred to as REO. When you buy a property at an auction, you have to pay at least the loan balance plus any interest and other fees accumulated during the foreclosure process. You also get the property 'as is,' which could include any liens or even its occupants. A REO sale is usually cleaner. The bank will remove liens, evict occupants, if needed, and generally prepare for the issuance of a title insurance policy to the buyer at closing. That said, REOs might be exempt from normal disclosure requirements. For instance, here in California banks are exempt from giving a so-called 'Transfer Disclosure Statement,' which is a document that requires sellers to tell you about any defects they are aware of."

"So it's sort of 'as is' as well, or could be?" Nancy asked.

"Well, it depends. The banks aren't in the business of maintaining homes, which is why they try to sell them quickly. Some lenders do go to the trouble of fixing up a place before they list it, but that depends on the bank and the location. Some properties are listed below market value to get them sold, fast, while others may be listed at market if the bank is trying to recover any costs involved with the loan default. On this street alone the prices vary quite a bit depending on which bank is behind it."

"I saw that in Phoenix when I looked there last year," Ted said.

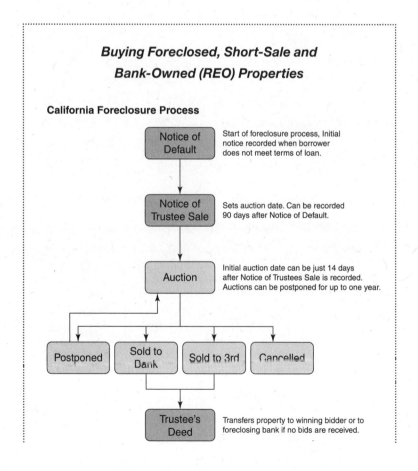

Buying Foreclosed, Short-Sale and Bank-Owned (REO) Properties

California Foreclosure Process

Notice of Default	Start of foreclosure process, Initial notice recorded when borrower does not meet terms of loan.
Notice of Trustee Sale	Sets auction date. Can be recorded 90 days after Notice of Default.
Auction	Initial auction date can be just 14 days after Notice of Trustees Sale is recorded. Auctions can be postponed for up to one year.

Postponed — Sold to Bank — Sold to 3rd — Cancelled

Trustee's Deed	Transfers property to winning bidder or to foreclosing bank if no bids are received.

Step 1- Notice of Default (NOD)

Properties are considered to be in pre-foreclosure from the filing of the initial Notice of Default until the property is sold at auction. During this period, the owner/borrower can cure the default by refinancing or working out a payment plan with the lender; a buyer can purchase the home directly from the owner; real estate agents can list the home and sell it for more than the amount due, or ask the lender to accept a short sale.

Step 2- Auction

After 90 days, there is generally a Notice of Trustee Sale filed, setting the auction date three weeks in the future. The notice must be advertised for three consecutive weeks. If the default is not cured by the sale date, the property goes to auction. Anyone can bid at the auction. However, the first bid amount will be equal to the outstanding loan balances plus fees and must be paid IN FULL by cashier's cheque at the actual auction.

Step 3- Unsold Property Reverts to Bank

If there are no bidders, the property reverts to the bank. Bank-owned properties are commonly referred to as REOs (Real Estate Owned). Buyers can try to purchase these properties directly from the bank, but, in general, the bank will list the property for sale with a real estate agent after evicting tenants and clearing liens. They will usually not do more than cursory repairs prior to putting the property on the market.

Foreclosed Properties

When a property owner is no longer able to make his mortgage payments and defaults on the loan, the property goes through a process known as foreclosure. When this occurs, the lender initiates the sale of the property by auction through a third party, called a trustee. The trustee is required to advertise a notice of default of the property in the newspaper for three continuous weeks. Take a look in the classified section of your local newspaper and you'll see a list of foreclosed properties for your area. The owner of the property has until five days before the scheduled date of the auction to pay all monies owed; if the owner cannot come up with the money within the allotted time period, the trustee conducts an auction for the property on the steps of a courthouse located in the county where the property is located. As previously stated, when buying a property during a foreclosure sale, you must pay at least the loan balance plus any interest and other fees accumulated during the foreclosure process. You must also be prepared to pay with cash in hand. And on top of all that, you'll receive the property 100% "as is." That could include existing liens and even current occupants who need to be evicted. Foreclosure auctions are particularly attractive to all-cash buyers and investors who are familiar with the process and are looking to get the most value for their investment dollar. However, many properties currently going through this process have little or no equity and will not sell for less than the current market value. Considering the property would come to the auction winner complete with tenants and senior liens, many properties revert to the bank and become REOs (see below).

Short Sale Property

A short sale property is a property being sold by an owner that is heading to foreclosure. The owner realizes that he can no longer afford the monthly payment and tries to sell the house before the lender completes the foreclosure process on the property. The term "short" means that the owner has listed the house for an amount which is less than the amount owed on the loan, the listing price being a reflection of current comparable properties in the area. As an example, let's say someone purchased a home two years ago with 100% financing for $680,000 in the middle of the hot real estate market. The home was purchased with an ARM (adjustable rate mortgage); the ARM matures after two years and the owner's mortgage payment jumps by $1,500 a month. In the meantime, the real estate market cools down, driving down prices of homes in the area. The owner is no longer able to make the house payment and decides to put the home up for sale. An appraisal on the home puts the value at $599,000. The owner is now upside down, owing more on the home than it's worth. He can't sell it for more than the current value of $599,000 so he's hoping the lender will cooperate with him and accept less than the full amount owed. In the short sale process, the lender has the authority to approve, deny or counter the submitted offer.

REO Properties

REO stands for "Real Estate Owned." These are properties that have gone through foreclosure and are now owned by the bank or mortgage company. This is not the same as a property up for foreclosure auction. When buying a property during a foreclosure sale, you must pay at least the loan balance plus any interest and other fees accumulated during the foreclosure process. You must also be prepared to pay with cash in hand. And, on top of all that, you'll receive the property 100% "as is." That could include existing liens and even current occupants that need to be evicted. An REO, by contrast, is a much "cleaner" and attractive transaction.

An REO property did not find a buyer during foreclosure auction. The bank now owns it. The bank will normally see to the removal of tax liens and mechanics' liens, evict occupants, if needed, and generally prepare for the issuance of a title insurance policy to the buyer at closing. Be aware that REOs are exempt from normal disclosure requirements like the Transfer Disclosure Statement—the document that requires sellers to tell you about any defects they are aware of.

Most buyers assume that any REO must be a bargain and an opportunity for easy money. This simply isn't true. You have to be very careful about buying an REO if your intent is to make money on it. While it's true that the bank is typically anxious to sell quickly, the bank is also strongly motivated to get as much as it can for the property. When considering the value of an REO, you need to look closely at comparable sales in the neighborhood and be sure to take into account the time and cost of any repairs or remodeling needed. The bargains with money-making potential exist, and many people do very well buying foreclosures. But there are also many REOs that are not good buys. This is where you have to do your homework to make sure the property you are interested in fits your needs.

Source: **www.lapropertysolutions.com**.

"You are also looking in Phoenix?" Paul asked.

"We aren't 100 per cent sure yet if we want a lifestyle purchase in a place like this, or an investment property in a place like Phoenix, where there's more year-round rental opportunity," Ted said. "Nancy is leaning towards the investment, but I'm stuck on the lifestyle property. If we buy here, we can rent it out and live it in when we're older."

"That's right," Paul said. "Of course, it's your decision, but if rental is what you are looking for, I would recommend we look at some homes in more populated parts of the city. You can buy here, of course, but it might be better in the shorter term to locate near one of the medical centers or a golf course."

"I think that might be best," Nancy said. "I know we haven't seen the house on this street yet, but I'm pretty sure I am not interested in buying in this area. There aren't enough people around, and it looks like it could be awhile before this becomes some kind of thriving community."

Ted nodded in agreement. "But we're here now, so let's look inside, just for fun."

Nancy agreed and Paul pulled up in front of a three-bedroom home with a two-car garage and a swing set in the back yard. Paul was right; the yard needed work, with dead shrubs and a pile of dirt in the back yard and a dead tree in the front. Inside, the home was mostly empty with the exception of some curtains left behind and a child's tricycle in the back yard. Paul and Ted's family did a quick tour of the entire house and within minutes were back in the car on their way to see some other listings Paul had set up.

Their next stop was a pair of townhouses in a gated community in Palm Desert. Nancy liked the building and the location. Ted was especially keen on the unit that overlooked the golf course. As they stood on the outdoor patio, three golfers approached the tee box a few hundred yards to the left.

"This doesn't look too safe," Nancy said.

Paul picked up on the concern as Nancy stepped in behind the fence that divides the townhouses.

"Oh don't worry, we're well off their path, Nancy. Golfers won't be hitting balls in here," Paul said.

"You obviously haven't seen my husband play, then," Nancy said, smiling at Ted who pretended not to hear.

Ted instead asked a question: "Paul, what is a unit like this worth, and could you rent it out fairly easily?"

"You might be able to pick up a two-bed unit for about $200,000," Paul said. "But the rent is a little trickier on a unit like this. You may not get them year-round."

Ted piped up: "I've also heard that if you go the short-term rental route, that the property management fees could be a lot higher than the standard 10 to 15 per cent?"

"That sounds about right. Someone has been doing their homework," Paul replied. Ted took it as a compliment.

They left the townhouse, and as they stood in the court-yard next to the "open house" sign, a couple a few years older than Ted and Nancy approached.

"Are you looking at buying a place in here?" asked the man, who introduced himself as Charlie from Edmonton.

"We are just looking. I'm Ted, this is my wife Nancy; we're from Vancouver. Why are you selling?" Ted said.

"Well, to be truthful we are looking for some good renters. I just wanted to see if you'd be interested in spending some time down here before you buy. We have a great place just a few doors down from here. We could give you a great deal. Interested?"

Ted paused and Paul looked a bit uncomfortable. Nancy then broke the silence: "Thank you very much for the offer, but we are really not 100 per cent sure if we are buying here yet. But we really appreciate you asking us. I'm sure your place is lovely."

Charlie and his wife thanked them for their time, apologized for interrupting and went on their way.

"Well, that doesn't bode well for my trying to show you a good place that you can buy, then rent, does it? Paul said.

"Don't worry, Paul," Ted said, slapping him on the back. "We aren't going to base our decision on one random conversation. How about we look at the next place?"

The next and final property Paul showed them was on the other side of the valley. It was a quaint rancher home that wasn't bank owned or broken down, it was just a family who were planning to move to a bigger home nearby. As they walked through the house, Nancy had a good feeling about the sellers, who had pictures of their children's paintings posted on the fridge, laundry piled neatly in the closets and family photos covering the mantel in the living room.

"Nice place," Nancy said. "And it looks like they've taken good care of it. What's wrong with it?"

"Nothing," Paul said. "I mean, I haven't done a home inspection, so there might be a few issues here and there—only an inspector can tell you that officially—but there's no sob story, no banks breathing down anyone's neck to sell. It's just a family looking for more room to grow."

Ted wandered off to the garage that was connected by a door through the kitchen, while Nancy inspected the back yard. She then went to find Ted, who was still in the garage admiring the tools organized by size across a large drafting table and hung in straight rows along the walls.

"Now, this is impressive," Ted said to Nancy as she walked towards him. He was staring at the garage as though it were a shrine.

"If they throw this in, I'll take it," Ted said.

"I hope you're joking," Nancy said.

"Yes, I'm just kidding, sweetie," Ted said, throwing his arm around her shoulder. "What do you think?"

"It's lovely, but I don't think it's for us. It's a little far from anything. There aren't any shops, parks or public transportation nearby," Nancy said. "In fact, I think we should get going. I'm exhausted."

Paul and Susie came into the garage together.

"What do you think?" Paul asked.

"I think we have a lot of good options to consider," said Nancy. "Thanks so much for your time with us today. Do you mind taking us back to our vehicle now? I'm wiped. It has been a long day."

As they drove back, Paul described some of the features of the Coachella Valley, which includes Palm Springs, Palm Desert, Rancho Mirage ("That's where the Betty Ford clinic is. I'm sure you've heard of that," Paul said), as well as La Quinta and Indio.

"One thing about Indio and the surrounding area that you have to be aware of is the wind storms that come through the valley. The Santa Ana winds. Have you heard of them?"

"I think I remember that from the last time we were here," Nancy said. "I had almost forgotten about that."

"It's just something to be aware of if you plan to spend any time here," Paul said.

The Santa Anas

The Santa Ana winds are strong, extremely dry offshore winds that characteristically sweep through southern California and northern Baja California in late fall into winter. They can range from hot to cold, depending on the prevailing temperatures in the source regions, the Great Basin and upper Mojave Desert. However, the winds are remembered most for the hot dry weather (often the hottest of the year) that they bring in the fall.

The air from the high desert is initially relatively dense, owing to its coolness and aridity, and thus tends to channel down the valleys and canyons in gusts that can attain hurricane force at times. As it descends, the air not only becomes drier, but also warms adiabatically by compression. The southern California coastal region gets some of its hottest weather of the year during autumn while Santa Ana winds are blowing. During Santa Ana conditions, it is typically hotter along the coast than in the deserts.

While characteristically hot and dry, the Santa Anas can also blow cold and dry, and in fact can bring some of southern California's coldest weather. High cloudiness, most commonly cirrus and altostratus, but also lenticular clouds may be observed, and on rare occasions these usually dry southwest-flowing winds can bring rain.

In the Los Angeles Basin, the winds are often credited with the extremely high visibility experienced in the area during the winter, in contrast to the hazy, smoggy summers. The adverse pulmonary health impacts have been understood by local doctors for decades; the winds pick up and transmit grit, dust, pollens, mold spores and other irritants and allergens for considerable distances. Residents regularly notice a build-up of dust in their homes and grit on their properties during these periods, which are frequent during the winter.

Source: **www.wikipedia.org**.

As they pulled into the parking lot at Paul's office, Ted asked if there was a difference between Canadian and US buyers.

"Are we really more polite? That's what we hear about ourselves, but I'm not sure if that's really true," Ted said.

"Well, first of all, and I'm not just saying this because you're sitting next to me, but yes, you are definitely more polite," Paul said. "But I get a few polite American clients, too. One thing I will say is that Canadians are more loyal to their real estate agents than Americans. I'm not saying this to make you commit to me—although that would be just fine by me—but Americans seem to have a handful of agents, whereas it seems to me Canadians see a few at first, then stick with the one they like the best."

Paul then explained that, despite what many Canadians think at first, the real estate process in America isn't a whole lot different, at least from what he has heard from Canadian clients.

"A lot of Canadians think it's difficult to buy a property down here, that we have a big sales tax when you buy a house and that our process is very difficult and you have to be here for closing. None of that applies at all," said Paul. "We have no sales tax when you buy a home, you don't have to be here for the closing and the seller pays all closing costs except notary or escrow cost, which is about 1 per cent of the price."

Paul talked about a few recent clients from Canada. "I was really busy when your dollar was at par with ours back in 2007 there. Canadians were flocking down here looking for places. I still get a lot of Canadian customers, but then, about 80 per cent of my clients were from there. A lot of people from Vancouver too," Paul said.

"It's not a bad commute from here to there. Travel time is an important factor if you are buying a lifestyle property, and even an investment one," said Paul.

Ted and Nancy said they agreed.

As they parted ways, Paul shook hands with Ted and Nancy and patted Susie on the head.

"We'll be in touch," Nancy said.

Ted gave Paul a soldier's salute. "Thanks for navigating us around this area, captain."

"Any time, mate," Paul said and waved goodbye.

The Coachella Valley

The Coachella Valley is a large valley landform in southern California populated by nearly one million people, and which includes the famed tourist destination, Palm Springs. The valley is bounded on the west by the San Jacinto Mountains and the Santa Rosa Mountains and on the north and east by the Little San Bernardino Mountains. The San Andreas Fault crosses the valley from the Chocolate Mountains in the southeast corner and along the centerline of the Little San Bernardinos. The Chocolate Mountains are home to a United States Navy live gunnery range and are mostly off-limits to the public.

A retirement haven throughout the area's history, senior citizens and the wealthy came to live in the Coachella Valley and a large percentage of residents are age 65 or older.

Daily high temperatures in the summer rarely go lower than 105° F. In winter, the temperatures range from 50° F (10° C) to 80° F (27° C), making it a popular winter resort destination.

The valley's northwest entrance from the Inland Empire along Interstate 10 is known as the San Gorgonio Pass and is one of the windiest places on earth. Cool coastal air

---

is forced through the pass and mixes with the hot desert air, making the San Gorgonio Pass one of only three ideal places in California for steady, wind-generated electricity. At the San Gorgonio Pass Wind Farm, hundreds of huge wind turbines spread across the desert and hills on either side of the highway greet visitors as they approach the crest of the pass and have become somewhat of a symbol of the area.

More than 200 golf courses blanket the area, making it one of the world's premier golf destinations. The Merrill Lynch Skins Game is held in La Quinta each Thanksgiving and draws some of the biggest names in golf. The PGA has a major presence in La Quinta as well with the PGA West golf and residential complex. One of the host courses of the Bob Hope Chrysler Classic, one of PGA West's fairways represents the area in Soarin' Over California, an IMAX-based attraction at Disney's California Adventure theme park.

Palm Springs is home to one of the country's largest collections of mid-century architecture. Thousands of homes, apartments, hotels, businesses and other buildings were designed in this fashion across the city. International mid-century enthusiasts come to Palm Springs to admire the design.

Source: **www.wikipedia.org**.

VIVA LAS VEGAS

Just after 11 p.m., Ted, Nancy and Susie drove into Las Vegas. Nancy turned to Susie, who was sleeping in the back seat, and gave her a gentle shake.

"Susie, wake up. We're in Las Vegas. You have to see all the lights."

Susie's one eyelid flipped open, then the other. Her eyes grew wide with excitement as the flashing red, and green lights of the city reflected across her face.

"Wow, they must have a huge hydro bill here!" Susie said.

Ted and Nancy laughed.

"Kind of makes us nagging you about turning out the lights seem kind of silly, doesn't it?" Ted said.

They pulled into the hotel parking lot and were greeted by a couple of employees. Ted, who had visited Las Vegas previously with his buddies, commented on how "dead" the place was compared to his last visit years before. "Money was falling out of people's pockets then," Ted recalled.

Ted headed to the counter to check in and Susie, still a bit sleepy, took a 360-degree look at the opulent surroundings.

"This place is tacky," said Susie.

Nancy laughed. "I agree with you, but your dad loves it here. It'll be fun. You'll see tomorrow. There's lot of stuff to see here."

They found their room and, after a long day of driving and sightseeing flopped onto their beds for the night, exhausted. Susie didn't even bother to change her clothes and crawled under the covers of her bed, which was located across the room from Ted and Nancy's. After settling into bed, Ted pulled out an ad they found online about the auction they were attending the next day.

"It says here the list prices range from $75,000 for a two-bedroom, 770-square-foot condo to $993,000 for a five-bedroom, 4,500-square-foot home. Most homes are in the mid-$100,000s to $300,000s,'" he told Nancy, who was lying down beside him.

"I wonder how far away this place is from where we are now?"

"Probably not close," said Nancy, who had her head on the pillow and eyes closed. "Let's worry about it tomorrow."

Ted tossed the paper on the floor and switched off the light.

"Good night, Nancy."

"Good night, Ted."

"Hey Nancy, I wonder . . ."

"Good night, Ted."

"Good night, sweetie," he replied and rolled over.

Las Vegas

Las Vegas is the most populous city in the US state of Nevada and an internationally renowned major resort city for gambling, shopping, fine dining and entertainment. The city bills itself as The Entertainment Capital of the World and is famous for the number of casino resorts and associated entertainment.

Established in 1905, Las Vegas officially became a city in 1911. With the growth that followed, at the close of the century Las Vegas was the most populous American city founded in the 20th century (a distinction held by Chicago in the 19th century). The city's tolerance for various forms of adult entertainment earned it the title of Sin City, and this image has made Las Vegas a popular setting for films and television programs. Outdoor lighting displays are everywhere on the Las Vegas Strip and are seen elsewhere in the city as well. As seen from space, the Las Vegas metropolitan area is the brightest on Earth.

Las Vegas enjoys abundant sunshine year round and has about an average of 300 sunshine days a year, with very little rainfall. The summer months of June through September are very hot and mostly dry with average daytime highs of 94 to 104° F and nighttime lows of 69 to 78° F. Most days in July and August exceed 100° F (38° C) but with very low humidity, frequently less than 10 per cent.

Las Vegas' winters are short and the season is generally mild, with daytime highs near 60 degrees and nighttime lows around 40 degrees. The mountains surrounding Las Vegas accumulate snow during the winter, but snow is rare in the Las Vegas Valley itself.

Annual precipitation in Las Vegas is about 4.5 inches (114 mm), which mainly occurs during winter but is not uncommon any time of the year.

Source: **www.wikipedia.org**.

At 8 a.m. the next day, Ted barreled into the hotel room and woke up Susie and Nancy, who were still sleeping.

"Come on, guys, let's get ready, time to go. We've got an auction to go to!"

Nancy sat up and looked over at Ted in disbelief.

"Are you kidding me? You're up already? Did you just come in the room? Where have you been?"

"I've been up since 5:30. I've showered, had breakfast and I was in the business center and printed out a bunch of stuff on the auction we're going to in . . ." Ted looked down at his watch. "Four hours! It'll take us a while to find the place and . . ."

"Hold on there, Ted. Slow down," Nancy said. "You've been up since 5:30? And you ate without us?"

"Nancy, I had a lot to do this morning. I still have to go get us a map so we can find this place where the auction is. The concierge said it might take us about 45 minutes to get there."

Nancy threw the covers off her bed and headed to the bathroom. Susie stretched her arms out from under the sheets and yawned.

"Okay, Dad, we're getting up, but you promised we'd only go for a little while, right? You said we could go to the Adventuredome later, remember?"

"Yes, Susie, I remember," Ted said and gave Susie a hug. "Now go get dressed and brush your teeth and let's go! The sooner we leave, the sooner we'll get to the amusement park!"

Susie jumped out of bed and into the bathroom and got ready alongside Nancy. To quicken the process, Ted took breakfast orders from each of them and headed down to the restaurant and ordered the food to go.

ON THE AUCTION BLOCK

Ted pulled into the parking lot at the site of the auction. There were hundreds of cars and dozens of people heading into the building, which looked like a mini convention centre.

"Wow, it's like a rock concert!" Ted said.

"Hardly," Nancy said. "More like Boxing Day at Wal-Mart. Let's get this over with."

"Nancy, don't be too quick to dismiss this auction process," Ted said. "We likely aren't buying here, but I've heard you can get some amazing deals at these things. Who knows, we might end up buying through one of these. It's not out of the question."

"Let's just see what it's about," Nancy said and grabbed Susie's hand. "Susie, stick by me the entire time okay? No wandering off, please."

"Okay, Mum," Susie said.

As they walked into the building, Ted spotted the registration desk for the auction. "I'll go check it out; you guys wait right here." Ten minutes later, he returned with a handful of pamphlets.

Purchasing a Property at Auction

If you plan to purchase a property at an auction, you must:

- Have a $5,000 cashier's check made payable to yourself, or cash.
- The available funds to write a personal check or pay cash for the balance of the required 5% earnest money deposit due on auction day.
- Valid picture identification for all parties to the transaction.

Source: Real Estate Disposition, LLC, **www.auction.com**.

"Okay, here's the deal: Registration is free and admission is free. Because we aren't buying today, we aren't guaranteed a spot, but they said this one isn't that busy so there should be lots of space."

"What happens if we were buying? Out of curiosity? Nancy asked.

Ted turned to one of the pamphlets in his hand.

"Well, according to this, it's all free, but if you are buying something you're required to bring a five-thousand dollar cashier's check—payable to yourself—as a deposit. You also need identification and all that. Also, they said it happens really fast, and that it's pretty exciting to watch."

"Well, I guess Susie and I will be the judge of that, won't we?" Nancy said. Susie smiled and nodded.

A few minutes later, a woman in a blue suit and badge waved at Ted.

"Oh, they said they would let me know if we're good to go in," Ted said. "Looks like we're good."

"What are you doing?" Nancy asked Ted, who suddenly had his head buried in his cell phone.

"I'm sending Sid a text to tell him we're at an auction, he won't . . ."

Nancy interrupted. "Make sure you tell him we are not buying or he will flip out."

"Good idea," Ted said, and then typed the words "Just looking," into his phone and hit send.

As they entered the room, Ted turned to Susie and Nancy and explained that the auction didn't start for another half hour, but first they held a bidding seminar and practice auction, to give participants a feel for how it worked.

"See, it's a good thing we got here early, isn't it?" Ted asked. Nancy and Susie were silent.

They took a seat at the back of the auditorium. In front of them were about 500 chairs, about half of them occupied. At the front was a stage with a podium. Over the loudspeaker, a voice introduced the people running the auction and they began explaining the process: "When a property you want to buy comes up, you raise your bidder's card high to be acknowledged. If you are the highest bidder, the auctioneer bangs his gavel and yells 'Sold!'" a man at the podium said.

He then explained that a 5 per cent "buyer's premium" would be added to all winning bid amounts to establish the total purchase price. That meant if your $200,000 bid was accepted, the total purchase price would be $210,000. Other specifics were also discussed, and anyone with questions was encouraged to ask the auction company's staff wearing the red vests throughout the room.

"Wow, sounds pretty efficient, doesn't it?" Ted said to Nancy. He then showed her a sample sheet he printed off the Internet:

Bidding at an Auction

Example

Winning Bid Amount = $300,000, plus $15,000 Buyer's Premium (5% of the winning bid amount) = Total Purchase Price of $315,000. Total interest money deposit due on auction day is 5% of the total purchase price = $15,750 (5% of $315,000). After crediting your cashier's check of $5,000 = $10,750 remaining to be paid by personal cheque or cash on auction day.

Tips for Bidders

Pay no attention to the starting bid price because tho final auction prices often end nowhere close to what the auction starts at. It's like selling a Nintendo Wii on Ebay with a starting bid of $1 or $150, because regardless of what you start it at, the Wii should be getting fair market value.

Make sure to check out the properties you're interested in before bidding. Bidding based on the square footage or the lot size only takes you so far because there may be underlying reasons why the home is being sold. If you visit a home and it has more damage than previously expected, you might not be so comfortable bidding on that particular property. Purchasing a home is an important life decision and it needs to be thoroughly researched beforehand.

Source: Real Estate Disposition, LLC, **www.auction.com**.

"What types of properties are these, and who owns them?" Nancy asked.

"Well, it's my understanding that they're everything from houses and condos to multi-family buildings," Ted said. "As for who owns them, it's the banks or other lenders who bought them through foreclosure or sales like that, from people who can't afford them anymore. The banks don't want to be in the real estate business, so they sell the homes at auctions like this to get rid of them, fast."

"Makes sense, I guess," Nancy said. "But it's so awful. I mean, families being pushed out of their homes."

"I know, it's not pretty," Ted said. "But maybe some of these families shouldn't have bought them in the first place. You know how it was down here for a while. If you had a pulse you could get a mortgage. George Bush's dream—that everyone could have his or her own home. I guess that dream turned into a bit of a nightmare."

"I feel like a vulture," Nancy said.

"Nancy, no matter how we buy a home, there's a pretty good chance we could be buying it from someone who didn't really want to sell it."

"I guess," Nancy said. "So, how do they know how much to ask for the homes?

"Well, this brochure here has that information, and a bit more. Check it out," Ted said and handed the paper to Nancy.

Auction Q&A

Question: How were the values determined? How current are they?

Answer: The previously valued price is based on the higher of A) the appraised value of the property in connection with the most recent mortgage on the property, B) the most recent asking price, C) the assessed value, or D) the most recent broker price opinion.

Question: Should I go inspect the property prior to bidding at the auction?

Answer: Yes, yes, yes! The only way for you to make an informed decision when it comes to bidding and buying is not only to visit, view and inspect the property prior to the auction, but also to read and review any property information and disclosure documents pertaining to that property. Do your investigation. Make your inspections. By registering and bidding at the auction, you are representing that you have not only viewed the property prior to bidding, but have also inspected, reviewed and accepted all relevant property information you deem necessary to make an informed decision. The properties will not be open for inspection after the auction, so be diligent and do your inspections and investigations beforehand.

Question: Can I conduct inspections after the auction?

Answer: No. All inspections must be completed prior to the auction. For each auction, there are select open house viewing dates for you to see the properties. They will not be open for walkthroughs or inspections after the auction.

Question: Can I bring a contractor with me during inspection?

Answer: Yes!

Source: **www.auction.com**.

After about an hour, Ted's eyes were glued to the auction process while Nancy was getting bored and Susie was asleep on her chair.

"I don't like how fast this is all happening," said Nancy. "I'm not sure this is for me. I need time to make decisions."

"It just looks fast, Nancy," Ted said. "And remember, these people have seen the houses beforehand; they know what they are getting into."

"Presumably," said Nancy. "I've read stories about buyers overseas buying dozens of houses they've never set foot in. That's scary."

"Well, we're not going to do it like that, don't worry," said Ted. "But if you guys want to go, we can leave."

"You promised Susie some fun time and that amusement park closes at 6:00, so we better get going now," Nancy said. She woke Susie and they headed out of the auditorium and back to the parking lot.

"I thought that was really interesting," Ted said.

"It was, actually," Nancy said. "I think we learned a lot about how that's done. You hear about it all the time, but I've never been to a housing auction before. In fact, I've never been to an auction, period. Good idea, Ted."

Ted smiled as they stepped back into the car and drove off to the indoor theme park. He promised Susie that they would spend some time in Las Vegas doing "Susie stuff" before heading to the Grand Canyon.

"Yeah! Finally," said Susie.

Suddenly Ted's phone vibrated from inside his shirt pocket.

"That must be Sid," Ted said, and flipped open the phone to read the response.

"This should be interesting," Nancy said sarcastically.

Ted then read the text from Sid out loud.

"Don't get caught up in the rush of the auction and make a big mistake. These things are designed to get you to part with money and each property is presented like it's the last one available in the world. I'm glad Nancy is with you."

"Here, here," said Nancy.

The phone vibrated again. It was Sid, again. Ted read it out loud, again.

"I have a buddy who bought a place down there as an investment and it's doing very well. He paid $160,000 for a townhome in an up-and-coming area and he's getting about $1,000 a month rent for it. I think it's cash flowing over $200 per month. Give me a call for a chat when you can. Sid."

6 Steps to Buying a Home at Auction

Step 1: Find and file properties.

Step 2: Confirm auction status.

Step 3: Check potential bargain.

Step 4: Determine bid amount.

Step 5: Bid at the auction.

Step 6: Take ownership.

STEP #1 - Find and File Properties

It's important to get up-to-date auction information and act on it as quickly as possible. Develop a system to keep track of properties that interest you. After you find a property online, it's a good idea to drive by to get a better idea of its condition and the type of neighborhood. For some buyers and investors, driving by the property has also facilitated a casual meeting with the owner (you may be able still to work out a last-minute deal before the auction) or yielded a wealth of unexpected information from a talkative neighbor.

STEP #2 - Confirm Auction Status, Location and Bidding Procedure

After a property is scheduled for auction, the owner has a chance (typically less than a month) to stop the auction by paying the amount owed to the foreclosing lender. It's also common for auctions to be postponed without a new date being published. Although cancellations and post-ponements are announced at the time and location of the originally scheduled auction, you can call the trustee to find out beforehand. Most auctions are at a public place in the same county where the property is located.

In many states, all the auctions in each county are at the same location. If you call the county clerk, make sure you clarify that you are looking for the location of *mortgage foreclosure auctions*, not *tax foreclosure auctions*. The bidding procedure varies from state to state, so you should become familiar with the procedure in your area before bidding at an auction. In some states, bidders are required to bring the full amount they want to bid in the form of cash or cashier's check to the auction. In other states, bidders are required to bring a certain percentage (10% is common) of the bid amount to the auction and pay the remainder within a certain timeframe if theirs is the winning bid. If you get a friendly representative when you call the trustee, you might be able to get information about how the bidding works in your area. But in most cases, you'll need to educate yourself. You can get started by reading RealtyTrac's state foreclosure laws. You could also contact a local real estate agent or attorney in your area. Of course, the best education will come from simply observing a local auction.

STEP #3 - Check Out a Potential Bargain

You need to find out as much as you can about the estimated market value of the property, how much is owed and if the owner has any other liens against the property. This is all public information and you can research on your own with the county recorder, or you can use RealtyTrac's property reports and tools to help.

The opening bid at the auction is based on the total amount owed to the foreclosing lender, and may include fees incurred because of the foreclosure proceedings. If no one bids above that amount, the foreclosing lender will take possession of the property. It's important to know this amount so you can determine if the auction represents a potential bargain purchase when the opening bid is compared to the property's market value.

If there are outstanding liens on the property, the winning bidder may be responsible to satisfy these, so it's important to check for any liens and the priority of the liens before you bid at the auction. A real estate attorney or title company can check for liens, or you can check directly with county records. The priority of a lien is usually determined by the date it was placed on the property. A first mortgage will usually have the first priority, and all other liens will be considered junior liens. In most states, the public auction clears out any junior liens, but there are exceptions such as tax liens, which typically will continue to be in effect after the auction.

STEP #4 - Determine Bid Amount

Based on all the factors used to determine the potential bargain—and your financial capability—you'll need to determine how much you can and should bid at the auction. Determining your bid amount is more obviously important in states where bidders are required to bring the full amount in cash or cashier's check. You won't even be qualified to bid if you don't meet that requirement. If you don't have that type of cash lying around, you have a couple options. If you own a home, you might be able to take out a Home Equity Line of Credit, which is a cash loan. If you can't secure a cash loan, you may consider trying to buy a pre-foreclosure or bank-owned property, both cases where you can usually obtain a regular mortgage loan secured by the property being purchased.

It's also important to determine the bid amount even in states where you don't need to bring the full amount to the auction. By setting a firm ceiling for your bid, you'll avoid getting caught up in the heady auction atmosphere and overbidding, which can result in little or no bargain for you. Also, if you're not able to pay the remainder of the bid within the time frame stipulated by state law, the deposit you paid at the auction is often nonrefundable.

A reasonable purchase amount at auction is at least 20% below full market value, and much better deals are often possible. Other factors to consider are the rate of real estate appreciation in the area and the potential for increasing the property's value by making repairs and improvements.

STEP #5 - Bid at the Auction

Call the trustee the day before or the day of the auction to check one last time if the auction has been canceled or postponed. If an auction is postponed, the trustee should provide the new auction date.

Arrive at the auction location early and locate the auctioneer as quickly as possible. Bidding at an auction can be intimidating, especially if you've never done it before. Take as many cues from the other participants as you can, but don't let them dictate how much you bid. You may encounter investors who attend many auctions every month and who don't necessarily appreciate new competition.

STEP #6 - Take Ownership

If you are the winning bidder, make sure you get the necessary documents from the auctioneer to verify that you are the winning bidder. Clarify with the auctioneer and a real estate attorney what further steps need to be taken before you take ownership and possession of the property. In some states, ownership can be transferred immediately or within a few days. In other states, you may need to wait a month or more for the sale to be confirmed by a court. Some states have redemption periods for the owner, in which case the owner can buy the property back from you if they pay the full amount paid at the auction, plus applicable fees. You should avoid spending money on repairs or improvements during the redemption period. If the trustee doesn't evict the current owners, you may be responsible to do this. If eviction is necessary, you can contact a local real estate attorney or the county sheriff for the proper procedure.

Source: RealtyTrac, **http://www.realtytrac.com/foreclosure/auc tion/how-to-buy-homes-at-auction.html**.

THE GRAND CANYON

Ted paid the expensive admission fee for the Grand Canyon Skywalk as Nancy and Susie stared in awe at the vast valley ahead of them. It was 27 Celsius, sunny with barely a cloud in the sky.

"My gosh," Nancy gasped. "It's even more beautiful than I imagined. And we really lucked out with the weather."

Susie was speechless as she continued to soak in the scenery.

Ted tucked his wallet into the back pocket of his shorts and led the three of them to the Skywalk perched 1,220 meters above the floor of the Grand Canyon, protruding 20 meters from the edge.

"I'm not even going to complain about how much that just cost," Ted whispered to Nancy about the skywalk fare.

"I know, it was a lot, but this is one part of the trip I've really been looking forward to," Nancy said. "I read a lot about this structure. It's been pretty controversial."

Susie seemed a bit scared by the height, but hung on tightly to her mother's hand as they walked the semi-circle.

"It's amazing," Ted said, as he looked across the horizon, and then at the gaping hole below.

"Sure is," said Nancy.

As they stared out at the amazing view, Ted turned to Nancy and said: "You know what this trip has made me realize, Nancy?"

"What's that, Ted?"

"Well, if we buy a vacation home in one place we would be restricting ourselves to visiting the same place," Ted said. "For example, I do want to visit Paris with Susie some day when she's old enough to brag about it to her friends. And I know, Nancy, you want to go to Ireland some day, and so do I. If we bought a lifestyle property now, it would be hard to justify taking flights to Europe when paying for a house down here somewhere."

"For a minute there, Ted, I thought you were going to say something romantic!" Nancy said, swatting him lightly with her hand. "But I am glad you are starting to see things from my point of view. Besides, as Susie gets older it will be fun to take her to different places. I know you were set on the idea of buying something just for personal use, but we can always do that later on in life."

Ted agreed. He then put one arm around Nancy and the other around Susie and pulled them close. The three stood in silence for a few minutes, gazing out at the gorgeous site before them.

THE NAPKIN ANALYSIS

At a diner along the highway where the three stopped for lunch, Nancy pulled a white napkin out of the silver container on the table and a pen out of her purse. She also pulled out her BlackBerry, logged on to the Internet and pulled up an online mortgage calculator.

"What's all that for?" Ted asked.

"I want to work out the difference between investing in a rental property and a lifestyle one," Nancy said, while drawing a chart on the napkin.

"But we don't have all the figures, Nancy," Ted said.

"I know, but let's just do some basic calculations to give us an idea of how it would differ. Let's consider some of the properties we've seen in the last few days," Nancy said, tapping away.

"For the investment property, I am going to use the place Sid mentioned in his text and for the lifestyle, the gated place in Palm Springs," said Nancy.

"But what about rents?" Ted asked.

"Well, for the investment, Sid mentioned around $1,000 and, of course, there would be no rent on the lifestyle, assuming we didn't rent it out. I have a mortgage calculator on a website here that we can use as well."

Ted sat back and studied the menu as Nancy continued to do calculations and fill in the blanks on a chart she drew on the napkin. Susie, meantime, was listening to her iPod and watching the different customers coming in and out of the restaurant.

"Okay, Ted, I am done," Nancy said.

"This is a little scary," she added, and pointed to the napkin analysis in front of her. She then spun it around for Ted to see up close.

"As you can see from these rough figures, the lifestyle option will cost us $11,592 a year, and that's BEFORE upkeep and all the travel costs of flying here and renting a car, etcetera. On the other hand, the investment option will cash-flow $2,724 a year."

"Wow!" Ted said. He then fell silent.

"Well there goes my three-day workweek idea and that trip to Paris, for sure."

"Now, we can see why Sid is so focused on investment property first and the lifestyle second."

Investment Property		Lifestyle Property	
Purchase price	$ 160,000	Purchase price	$ 200,000
Down payment	$ 40,000	Down payment	$ 50,000
Principal	$ 120,000	Principal	$ 150,000
Monthly rent	$ 1000	Monthly rent	$ —
Monthly mortgage @6%	$ 773	Monthly mortgage @6%	$ 966
Cash flow	$ + 227	Cash flow	$ - 966
Yearly cash flow	$ +2,724	Yearly cash flow	$ -11,592

The waitress, dressed in a red dress, white apron and white sneakers with a nametag that read "Hi, My Name is Cindy," walked up to the table. "What can I get you folks?" Cindy asked.

Ted, who was still in shock replied: "Bread and butter. No, in fact, just bread. We can't afford the butter."

TED'S TIPS

- Consider different types of property purchases, from regular sales to foreclosures, including auctions and bank-owned sales, but be aware of the conditions of each.

- When looking for property in a particular community, ask local residents about some of the pitfalls of living there, including weather patterns or area businesses that might "contribute to" lower property values or increased expenses to maintaining a property in the area.

- Take time out and have some fun while searching for real estate.

- Don't assume that the best deals are found at auctions. This is a misconception.

8

Of Phoenix and Palm Springs, and Narrowing the Search

As they drove into Phoenix, Nancy was taken aback by the urban sprawl. She then pulled out some printouts from her "Phoenix file" in her backpack and started reading off some facts about the city.

"Phoenix is home to a large number of parks and recreation areas. Many water parks are scattered around the valley to help residents cope with the harsh desert heat during the summer months. There's also an amusement park in north Phoenix."

"Yeah! Can we go?" Susie asked from the back seat. "I'm tired of looking at boring houses!"

"We can probably arrange that," said Ted. "After all, we're here for a few days, so we should have some time to play."

"Oh, look at that," said Nancy, pointing to a commuter train in the distance. "I read about that; it's a new light rail project that opened at the end of 2008. Where's the information on that? Oh, here. It is called the METRO Light Rail and runs from north-central Phoenix through downtown and then east to Tempe and Mesa."

Nancy turned to Ted. "That's a good boost for commuters. We should probably consider buying a place with good access to that, if we can."

Ted nodded. "Good idea. Let's tell the real estate agent about that."

"What time are we meeting him tomorrow?" Nancy asked.

"Ten," said Ted. "He's meeting us at a coffee shop across the street from where we're staying."

"How did you find this place where we're staying, again?" Nancy asked.

"The Internet," Ted replied. "I picked the one that seemed the most central, and the cheapest."

"Oh dear, that sounds like it could be really good, or really bad," Nancy said.

They eventually found the building where they would spend the next few nights. Ted picked up the keys from the security office and parked the car in the underground garage. When they opened the door to the suite, they were welcomed by a blast of air conditioning and the late-day sun streaming through the windows.

"This place looks good," Nancy said as she dropped her bag on the kitchen counter. Susie chose her bedroom and then ran to the bathroom, while Ted stood in front of the main window, his hands placed on his hips.

"Yeah, it's a nice spot. It has a good view. I can see the golf course just down the road there to the right. And I think there's a little complex down there with a grocery store and a coffee shop," Ted said, looking down.

"Good work, Ted," Nancy said. "Now, do you mind going back to the garage and getting the rest of the luggage?"

Ted groaned. He then grabbed the car keys and headed for the front door. Before he opened it, he noticed a sign taped to the back of the door.

"Hey, take a look at this," Ted said. Nancy walked towards him.

He read the sign: "Welcome to Phoenix and to our building. We are sure you will enjoy your stay. There are several amenities in the area. If you have any questions, feel free to call the property manager at the number below."

"What else does it say?" Nancy asked. "The note looks longer than that."

"Hold on, give me a minute," Ted said.

"It says, 'If you enjoyed your stay and are interested in buying this unit call John at . . .' Hey, that's a Vancouver number. The owners are from home!" Ted said, surprised.

"That's a coincidence," said Nancy. "I wonder what they are asking for it?"

"We should call them later and find out," Ted said.

"Let's just take it easy for today. We can call them tomorrow or the next day, maybe after we've seen a few places first," replied Nancy.

Ted agreed, and opened the door to leave and get the bags.

"Let's get Mexican food tonight!" he said as he walked out of the unit. "They've got great Mexican restaurants here!"

Phoenix, Arizona

Phoenix is the capital and largest city in Arizona, followed in size by Tucson and then four Phoenix metropolitan area cities of Mesa, Glendale, Chandler and Scottsdale.

Arizona is noted for its desert climate, exceptionally hot summers and mild winters, but the high country in the north features pine forests and mountain ranges with cooler weather than the lower deserts. Population figures for the year ending July 1, 2006 indicate that Arizona was at that time the fastest growing state in the United States, exceeding the growth of the previous leader, Nevada, and is currently the second.

Arizona is one of the Four Corners states. It borders New Mexico, Utah, Nevada and California, touches Colorado, and has a 389-mile (626-km) international border with the states of Sonora and Baja California in Mexico. In addition to the Grand Canyon, many other national forests, parks, monuments and Indian reservations are located in the state.

Source: **www.wikipedia.org**.

Facts about Arizona

- Arizona became the 48th state on February 14, 1912.
- A person from Arizona is called an Arizonan.
- Phoenix originated in 1866 as a hay camp to supply Camp McDowell.
- Arizona observes Mountain Standard Time on a year-round basis. The one exception is the Navajo Nation, located in the northeast corner of the state, which observes the daylight savings time change.

– The bola tie is the official state neckwear.
– The amount of copper on the roof of the Capitol building is equivalent to 4.8 million pennies.
– The state's precipitation varies. At Flagstaff the annual average is 18.31 inches; Phoenix averages 7.64 inches; and Yuma 3.27 inches.
– Blue and gold are the official state colors.
– Arizona is a right-to-work state. The law states no person shall be denied the opportunity to obtain or retain employment because of non-membership in a labor organization.
– The saguaro cactus blossom is the official state flower. The white flower blooms on the tips of the saguaro cactus during May and June. The saguaro is the largest American cactus.
– The Palo verde is the official state tree. Its name means green stick and it blooms a brilliant yellow-gold in April or May.
– The cactus wren is the official state bird. It grows seven to eight inches long and likes to build nests in the protection of thorny desert plants like the arms of the giant saguaro cactus.
– Arizona's most abundant mineral is copper.
– Four Corners is noted as the spot in the United States where a person can stand in four states at the same time.
– In 1939 architect Frank Lloyd Wright's studio, Taliesin West, was built near Phoenix.

Source: http://www.50states.com/facts/arizona.htm.

MEETING "SAM," THE REALTOR

At 10 a.m. sharp the next day, at a coffee shop across the street from their rental unit, a six-foot-tall redheaded woman wearing a beige suit and gold high-heel shoes approached Ted, Nancy and Susie. She had her hair pulled back tightly in a bun and was carrying a tan leather briefcase in one hand, a BlackBerry and set of keys with a BMW tag in the other. She put down her briefcase, pulled off her oversized sunglasses, stuck out her hand and introduced herself as Sam, the agent recommended to Ted by the brothers he met at the Suns game the last time he was in town.

Ted, with a surprised look on his face, shook Sam's hand.

"I'm Sam—Samantha," she said in a thick Texan accent. "I really do have to put my picture up on my website again. You're alright with a Texan woman showing you around the place, I assume?"

"Absolutely," said Ted, with a smile.

"It'll be nice to have a woman show us around for a change," said Nancy. "How long have you lived in Phoenix?"

"About 20 years now, but I haven't been able to shed the accent, as you can tell," said Sam. "My husband works with the Phoenix Suns, the basketball team. Ya'll heard of them?"

"I sure have," said Ted. "Can he get us tickets?"

"Ted!" Nancy shouted. "Ignore him," Nancy said to Sam.

"That's all right. I might be able to get you some tickets sometime, but let's get to know each other a little first. So, you said you have narrowed down your search to a townhome in a complex somewhere in a good rental area, with a good employment rate and a safe neighborhood, right? And your price range is about $150,000?"

"That's right," Nancy said. "We want something we can rent out year round, to a couple or family. Something that's clean and in a good area, but not too expensive, but that has some good demographics and might bounce back in price in the next five years or so."

Sam showed printouts of six properties she planned to show them that day.

"What I'd like to do is show you some units in a complex down the street from here. It's a great location and already has a few Canadian owners. One I know is a retired couple— lovely people. They live here for about four months a year. They bought in years ago. And I just sold a unit to some Canadians from Edmonton. They bought a place and are renting it out right now. They are retiring in a few years and plan to take it over then. There are a couple other units for sale in the building that we can look at. What do you say? Want to start there?"

"Sure," Ted said.

"Sounds good," added Nancy. Susie shook her head in agreement. "I like your shoes," she said to Sam.

"Thanks, Susie. I like your T-shirt," Sam said. It was black with "Las Vegas" written across the front in sparking letters.

"Thanks!" Susie said. "We just got back from there. It was fun, well, most of it was fun except for the auction we had to go to. I fell asleep."

"Well, we'll try to keep you entertained on this trip," Sam said with a huge smile.

"She's sweet," Sam said to Ted and Nancy.

As they got comfortable in the leather seats of Sam's BMW, she described to Ted and Nancy the different cities in Maricopa County, including Phoenix, Avondale, Chandler and Glendale and others.

"About 3.8 million people lived here as of mid-2007, which is fourth among the nation's counties and greater than the population of 24 states," Sam said. "In 2007, *Forbes* ranked four of Maricopa County's municipalities in the top 10 fastest-growing cities in the nation."

Ted raised his eyebrows and Nancy also looked impressed.

"That's good for rentals, right?" Ted said. "It's certainly better than a lot of places. We have our overbuilt parts, but in my opinion the demand is there if you're in the right location."

Sam pulled up to a complex in a gated community.

"This is the place I was telling you about," she said, then turned off the engine and walked them through the courtyard.

As they walked along, Ted and Nancy immediately noticed how well maintained the complex was. Sam said it was an area where many professionals live, and some tourists like to stay if they want to be closer to business centers and other professional services, as well as the airport and public transit. The prices ranged from $125,000 to $350,000, depending on the size and location of the units.

"Of course, that's down considerably from 2006," Sam said. "But some people have owned here since the place was built about 15 years ago."

Sam showed them two units for sale; one was a two-bedroom with an offer pending, which was closer to their price range, and the other was a recent listing with three bedrooms, two baths and slightly more than they wanted to spend. Ted and Nancy were impressed by the building, in particular the location, and the state-of-the-art alarm system.

"I like this," Nancy whispered to Ted as they left the second unit. "I think this is the kind of place we should be looking for."

She then turned to Sam: "What are the rents like in here? We are looking for an area with higher rents so we can make a bit of a monthly profit."

"Well, it depends on the number of bedrooms you buy, and the location in the building, but I'd say in here you can get about $750 a month for a one-bedroom and $1,300 for a two-bedroom."

Ted and Nancy looked at each other and nodded.

"What do you think? Is this along the lines of what you are looking for?" Sam asked.

"I think it is," Nancy said, while holding Susie's hand. "I think it's very close."

"Let me show you a couple more like this then," Sam said. "One is a bit higher priced and one is lower. I want to give you an idea of what you can get on either end of your price range."

"Sounds good," said Nancy.

DIGGING DEEPER

Later that evening at their suite, over take-out Chinese food, Ted and Nancy decided to do a little more digging around some of the neighborhoods in Phoenix.

"We should go back to that building we liked and talk to some of the neighbors," Ted said. "See what they say about the area."

"Do we have to?" asked Susie.

"I have an idea," said Nancy. "Why don't you go talk to the neighbors and I'll take Susie to Starbucks for a couple of iced drinks." Susie approved the plan and off they went.

The three stepped into Starbucks around the corner from the building they were considering.

"I like this one better than the last Starbucks we went to in that first city," Susie said.

"You mean Palm Springs?" Ted asked.

"Yeah," Susie said. "There were mostly Grandmas and Grandpas in that one. This one has some other kids at least."

Ted and Nancy laughed and nodded.

"She's right about that," Nancy said. "It's definitely a different demographic in this neighborhood than some we visited in Palm Springs."

"Generally, that's true. I guess it depends where you go," Ted said. "So, I'm going to go knock on a few doors, meet you guys back here in an hour?"

"Good plan. Meanwhile, Susie and I are going to go for a bit of a walk. I think I saw a park up the street. We'll check it out."

Do Your Research on Potential Rental Properties

The following are some tips on what to check out:

- Local papers for cost of rental units in the area. Call an owner looking to rent and interview them.
- Ask the building's property manager about vacancy rates.
- Local transportation access
- Condo fees
- Amenities in complex
- Shopping in the area
- Interview a resident about the pros and cons of the building.

> – Meet a local property management company and
>   ask what type of units are most in demand.
> – Consult local economic development office about
>   population growth in the area/neighborhood.
>
> Source: Philip McKernan Inc., **www.philipmckernan.com**.

FAREWELL PHOENIX, AGAIN

On their fourth and final day in Phoenix, after three days of house hunting, researching, sightseeing and taking Susie to the waterslides, Ted and Nancy were content. They had seen more than two dozen properties in two states, and were starting to really narrow their choices and what they wanted in a property.

"What do you think? Phoenix or Palm Springs?" Nancy asked over breakfast, watching with one eye how much syrup Susie had spread on her pancakes.

"It's a tough call," Ted replied while taking a scoop of his scrambled eggs. "They both have their advantages and disadvantages. I think Phoenix, from what we've seen, better suits our price range and the type of property we want, which is one to rent out year-round. I think there might be more demand for rental units here than in Palm Springs."

"So it's settled, then? Phoenix for an investment property?"

Ted nodded, his cheeks stuffed with food.

"I think we should work with Sam and ask her to keep an eye out for properties for us," Nancy said.

"Yes, I agree," Ted said.

"Also, have you talked to Sid lately?" Nancy asked.

"Oh, that reminds me," Ted said. "He sent me an email with a more detailed comparison of a lifestyle property versus an investment one. Check this out."

Ted unfolded a printout of the email and handed it to Nancy.

Cash Flow Comparable Tool

Using two different properties, each with 25% down payment and a 25-year amortization.

	Lifestyle Condo $150,000	Investment Condo $150,000
Mortgage @ 5%/month	$658	$658
Property Tax/month	$100	$100
Municipal Services (e.g. water, & sewer)/month	$100	$0 – Tenant
Condo fees/month	$150	$100
Management/month	N/A	$60
Repairs & Maintenance Allowance/month	$60	$60
Insurance/month	$80	$80
Vacancy Allowance/month		$60
TOTAL Monthly Costs	$1,148	$1,118
Annual costs	$13,776	$13,416
Monthly rental income	0	$1,195
Annual rental income	0	$14,340
Annual Cash flow	−$13,776	+ $924

Please note the samples above are before mortgage pay-down or equity appreciation.

Source: Pauline McKernan

"Nancy, have a look at all the fees and charges," Ted said. "I never thought of all of this extra stuff"

"It's good to see them laid out in detail like that," Nancy said. "It shows, once again, the cost of owning a lifestyle property. Just more proof that a lifestyle property might not be the right fit for us, at least not now. Did you see the note on the bottom about mortgage buy-down and equity appreciation, Ted?"

"Oh yeah, Sid asked me to call him to discuss this, as he said this is really important to take into consideration. Why don't I try him now?" Ted asked, dialing Sid's phone number.

Sid answered, and Ted filled him in on their progress. He asked for clarification about the note on the bottom of the cash flow tool.

"I can see you guys are really starting to see the difference between an investment and lifestyle property." Sid said, sounding like a proud father.

"So, about this chart," Ted continued. "The cash flow on the property is not quite as high as I expected. It will take forever for us to buy a lifestyle property from the profits from this one."

"Don't be discouraged, buddy," Sid said. "When buying an investment property, you must also look at two other key elements in addition to cash flow. Do you have a pen? You might want to write this down."

Ted rested the phone between his ear and shoulder and motioned to Nancy to hand him a pen and paper.

"Okay Sid, shoot. I'm writing it down," Ted said.

Sid continued. "The first thing to consider is equity appreciation. This is how much you think the property will go up in value, or not, over a period of time. What I do is use a conservative 5% per year, compounded. So if we look at the example

I gave you, in five years that property could be worth $41,442 more, and in 10 years an additional $94,334. Got that?" Sid asked.

"Yup," Ted said, writing furiously.

"The second is the mortgage pay-down," Sid said. "This is basically the money you pay off the mortgage. After five years, you will have paid down $12,847, and after 10 years $29,335. So guys, what this means is potentially you will have built up equity of $54,289 after five years and $123,669 after 10 years."

"Wow" Ted said. "I had never even thought of that before."

"I haven't finished yet, Ted," Sid said. "If you put a tenant in the property all year round, then they will also cover the running costs on the property as well."

"That sounds more like it," Ted said. "We get to buy a place have a tenant pay for the running costs, pay down our mortgage, give us some cash flow and the bonus is any capital appreciation we get."

"That's it in a nutshell," Sid said. "You learn fast now."

"Thanks again, buddy," Ted said.

"Thanks Sid!" Nancy shouted into the phone.

"You're welcome," Sid said. "Unfortunately, I have to run. Say hi to Nancy and Susie. We'll talk soon. Good luck!"

Ted then turned to Nancy and explained what Sid had outlined.

"It's good to see them laid out in detail like that," Nancy said. "It shows, once again, the cost of owning a lifestyle property. Just more proof that a lifestyle property might not be the right fit for us, at least not now."

Ted then paid the bill and they piled back into their vehicle and headed out of Phoenix towards Palm Springs, where they'd catch their flight home the next night.

Summary of Sid's capital appreciation and
mortgage pay-down

	5 year	10 year
Capital Appreciation	$41,442	$94,334
Mortgage Pay-Down	$12,847	$29,335
Total Equity	$54,289	$123,669

A RESORT BECKONS

About 40 miles out of Phoenix, Nancy noticed some large billboards on the side of the road for a resort called Mountain Springs.

"Hey, I saw a brochure for that place," Nancy said, pointing to the huge, newly-built complex. "Let's stop there."

Ted obliged. After all, he had to use the restroom. As they turned into the resort, they followed a long tree-lined driveway that took them to a large flower garden surrounding a huge water fountain. Ted immediately noticed the golf course to the right and a row of beautiful homes alongside it. As they drove towards the main entrance, Nancy noticed some smaller townhomes to the left, and an "open house" sign out front.

"Let's take a look," Nancy said with excitement in her voice.

This surprised Ted. He thought she was tired of property hunting. Not to mention, this was not her type of investment property.

As they entered the unit, both Ted and Nancy (and a reluctant Susie) were greeted by a young woman. She handed them a brochure and invited them to take a look around. As they strolled through the space, Nancy noticed the appliances and all of the fixtures were top of the line. Ted commented on the quality workmanship, and the expensive wood they used on the floors and doorways throughout. As they stepped into the master bedroom, Nancy immediately noticed it had a view of the mountains from across the golf course. She gasped.

"Oh my goodness," Nancy said. "This is beautiful."

Ted looked over at her. It looked as though she might cry.

"Are you okay?" he said.

"Yes," Nancy said, covering her mouth with both hands. "I just can't believe how gorgeous this place is!"

As they walked into the living area, a man named Roger introduced himself as the sales manager at the resort.

"So, what do you think?" Roger said.

"Nice place," Ted said.

"It's paradise," Nancy replied.

Ted looked at Nancy, a bit confused.

Roger explained to them more about the history of the resort, its features and surroundings. He told them the price range, from $250,000 to $500,000, depending on the unit and its location.

"If you want to stick around and get a feel for the place you can stay the night," Roger said. "It's on us. All you'd have to pay for is food and drink. We've got some great restaurants on site."

Ted shook his head. "No, thanks, we really should . . ."

"Sounds good. We'll stay," Nancy interrupted.

Ted shrugged and smiled. "I guess we're staying."

Roger asked them to sign in and gave them a key to a unit right next door to the one they had just visited. They grabbed their luggage from the SUV and settled in.

"Nancy, are you all right?" Ted said. "I am really surprised you wanted to stay here."

"Why wouldn't I?" Nancy asked. "I mean, look at this place."

After a swim in the pool and a nice dinner, Susie stayed in the room to watch a movie while Ted and Nancy took a short walk around the resort.

"Well, it's good to at least see a place like this. It's sort of a nice way to end the trip," Ted said. "Don't you think?"

"You know, Ted, it's not that expensive," Nancy said. "Maybe we should look into buying here?"

Ted stopped. He then put his hand on Nancy's forehead. "Do you have a fever?"

"No, Ted," she said, pushing his hand away. "Ted, this is the first place I've seen that I could say I would love to spend time in. For the first time, I get why having a lifestyle property would be a good idea. Think of how wonderful it would be to live in a place like this for a few weeks every year."

Ted realized Nancy was being serious. "You're not suggesting we buy here are you?"

"Yes," Nancy said. "I mean no, not really. But, why not?"

Ted grabbed Nancy's hand and pulled her towards a nearby bench to sit down. "Nancy, you sound like me a year ago. Maybe the heart and not the head . . ."

Nancy paused and sat quietly for a few minutes. She then sighed. "I know, I know," she said quietly. "It's like I'm doing the opposite of what I said we should be doing all along! I just want this. In five or so years from now, I want a place like this."

Ted put his arm around Nancy. "Tell you what. In five years we'll come back and look for a place like this, for us. But for now, I think we need that practical Nancy back. We're so close to making the right choice for us. Let's not throw our plan out the window."

Nancy nodded in agreement. "You're right, Ted. I know you're right."

The couple stood up and slowly walked back to their unit and went to bed.

As he pulled the sheets over him, Ted reflected on how much he learned in the past few months about property and his own goals. Knowledge really is power, he thought to himself, smiling.

Different Types of Real Estate

Lifestyle Property

A property that is purchased for personal or recreational use

Investment Property

Property purchased solely for future economic gain through cash flow and/or capital appreciation

Hybrid Property

To include property such as condominium hotels, deeded time-shares, rental pooled real estate, restricted owner usage and lifestyle real estate that is rented on an intermittent basis

Source: Philip McKernan Inc. **www.philipmckernan.com**.

Lifestyle Score Card

What to Look for in a Lifestyle Property

Location (Country)

Are you sure the US is the right location for you?

Have you traveled to many other countries apart from the US.?

Why the US over, say, the Caribbean?

Location (State)

Is the sun a major motivator?

Do you want to be near the ocean?

Do you prefer a dry dessert climate?

What average temperatures suit you?

Location (City)

Why the city you have chosen?

Have you visited it at least twice?

Can you *really* say you know it?

Direct flight to city?

Distance from airport?

Is there a time zone difference?

Transportation availability?

Property

Type of property

Do you want a townhouse?

Would you prefer a condo?

Is acreage an option?

Gated community?

What size do you need, as opposed to what you want?

Recreation

Do you want a golf course?

Private swimming pool or communal pool?

Gym in complex or nearby?

Barbeque?

Hot tub?

Community

Health

    Hospital?

    Dentist?

    Pharmacy?

Recreation

Shops and restaurants?

    Parks, trails, library?

    Theatres, video stores, museums and galleries?

    Professional sports teams/venues?

Source: Philip McKernan Inc. **www.philipmckernan.com**.

TED AND SID TALK IT OVER

On Sunday morning, the day after their March Break vacation and house-hunting, Ted called Sid to bring him up to speed on his and Nancy's decision to buy a property in Phoenix as an investment, and their new goal.

"What do you think of that?" Ted asked.

"That's great news. You're happy with that decision, then?" Sid asked.

"Yeah, I think so. I mean, yes, I am. It wasn't my idea going into this process. You know my idea was to buy a place where we could vacation. But Nancy has a point, that we might not want to vacation just there all the time. What do you think?"

"I think I'm proud of you, buddy. You had a goal, and then you pursued it, including weighing the pros and cons and doing some homework. You even visited a lot of places, which not a lot of people do."

"Well, it wasn't cheap," Ted said. "That's a lot of vacation money we used up in the last few months."

"Think of it as the price of due diligence, an investment in your investment," Sid replied. "So what's next?"

"Well, we think we have a great real estate agent in Phoenix, a Texan named Sam, and we've asked her to keep an eye out for us for a property in a complex that would have good rental opportunities."

"How soon are you looking to buy?"

"We're ready for whenever something comes up, I guess. We don't want to wait too long, but a few months would be nice just to save up a bit more money for the down payment."

"Well, the good news there is that, even if you bought tomorrow, the banks are so overwhelmed right now that the closing process is a bit slower than you might expect."

"That's good, I guess," Ted said. "Oh, that reminds me. We stayed in a unit in Phoenix that the owner was trying to sell. He's from Vancouver. I'm going to give him a call and see what he has to say."

"Was there something wrong with the unit?" Sid asked.

"I didn't notice anything. It was a good building, in a professional part of the city. Not a ton of character, but a decent place."

"Are you thinking of buying it?"

"I don't think so. I think we we're thinking of something in more of a residential area, and something a bit bigger, with more bedrooms. But I just want to see if he'll tell me something about what it's like down there to buy and rent out a place," Ted said.

"That's a smart idea. Let me know what he says," Sid said. "When you talk to him, focus on the cash flow and equity appreciation of certain areas. You want a property that not only spins off monthly profit, but has the potential to increase in value at a greater rate than other areas."

"We're all over that, Sid. Nancy and I have really been doing our homework."

"That's great, Ted. Keep me posted."

Ted then changed the subject. "So, I hear you and the family are coming out in July. That's great news. How long are you staying?"

"Long enough to beat you at the next round of Risk, my friend," Sid laughed.

"We'll see about that, buddy. I let you win last time. I won't be as cordial next time," Ted countered.

They laughed.

"Well, keep in touch Ted," Sid said. "Can't wait to hear more about what happens with the investment, and can't wait to see Nancy and Susie. You, well, that'll be okay too."

"Back at you, buddy," Ted said, and they both hung up the phone.

Ted then decided to call the seller of the unit where they stayed.

Equity Appreciation

Is the property also well positioned for appreciation? If you do enough due diligence, you can always find a stable market where you can get positive cash flow. The challenge is to find a property that not only spins off positive cash flow but also has the potential to increase in value at a greater rate than other areas. Ask yourself: Do you want to own a $100,000 property that goes up 4% per year or

6% per year? A profit of $100 per month helps you buy and keep the property, while $200 per month could help you retire sooner!

Source: Philip McKernan Inc., **www.philipmckernan.com**.

TED CALLS THE OWNER OF THE CONDO

On the third ring, Ted heard a voice at the other end of the phone: "Hello, Bruce here."

"Bruce! My name is Ted. I'm from Vancouver and I stayed in your condo in Phoenix recently. I noticed it's for sale and I have a few questions. Do you have a minute?"

"Ted, thanks for the call. Can you hang on one second?" Bruce asked.

Ted then heard muffled voices for a few seconds before Bruce returned to the line.

"Sorry Ted, just dropping my kids off at soccer practice. Making sure they got all the right equipment with them. You know how it is, maybe?" Bruce asked.

"Yup, got a daughter in soccer myself. She's 10. How old are yours?"

"Sixteen, twins, great girls," Bruce said. "So Ted, tell me, what can I do for you? Did you want to buy it?"

"Well, not exactly Bruce, I'm sorry," Ted said. "But would you mind answering a couple questions anyway?"

"Sure, why not, for a fellow soccer dad, I'd be happy to," Bruce said.

"Well, I was wondering why you're selling. I'm also curious about how successful you are at renting it out." Ted asked.

There was a brief pause on the other end of the line. Bruce cleared his throat.

"Well, Ted, the truth is we're looking at places in California. We're planning to retire in a couple years and the wife wants to live in more of a retirement town—something a little slower, like Palm Springs or Palm Desert. We have owned that Phoenix place for nearly a decade now; it's been good to us," Bruce said.

"Isn't that funny?" Ted said. "That's exactly what my wife and I are planning to do, although we're in the first half of that plan. We're buying in Phoenix, want to rent out the place for five or more years, and then buy our own retirement place, also in California. We were in Palm Springs last week in fact."

Bruce laughed. "Well, of course, I think that's a great plan!"

"Tell me more about renting it out?" Ted asked.

"Well, it was pretty easy at first, I have to say. You've seen the condo so you know it's a great location, and Phoenix was growing like gangbusters for a while there, something like 30 per cent population growth since the turn of the century. We didn't have much trouble renting year round. For the last couple of years, we've been taking the place for three months in the winter and renting it out the rest of the time. There's been a few months in the summer where we haven't had tenants, and it's getting tougher to rent it out now, so we've decided to sell and take a retirement place instead."

"It's not a great time to be a seller, though, is it?" Ted asked.

"It's not, but the wife and I thought if we can get a decent price and erase from our life the hassle of renting it out, we'd be further ahead both financially, but more importantly, mentally. It's a lot of work," Bruce said.

"What about the property rental companies? Don't they make it easy for you?" Ted asked.

"Sure, it's easy, but you also pay for their services. Some even charge you when you don't have tenants. You have to be careful with some of them. Read the fine print in the contract before you sign. That's my advice," said Bruce.

"That's good advice, thanks a lot Bruce," Ted said. "How's the sale going? Any offers so far?"

"Actually, I had an offer come in last night. I was hoping if you wanted it too I could have myself a little bidding war," Bruce laughed. "I think that's too much to ask. I'll just be happy for a reasonable price. We've done well by it over the years, so I'm happy."

"That's great, Bruce. Thanks again for your time, and I hope your daughters win their next game!" "Thanks, Ted," Bruce said. "Good to talk to you. Best of luck with your little soccer star as well."

How a Property Manager Is Able to Help You

These are the common and important tasks that you can rely on your property manager to do for you:

- Advertise and help you look for new tenants if your property is untenanted
- Interview, screen and choose your ideal tenants
- Collect rent from your tenants every month and handle late payments if there are any
- Help your tenants settle any complaints and issues that they have. If your tenants cause any problems

or trouble, your property manager will have to handle them as well.

- Repair any damages to your property, fixtures, furniture and appliances so you can maintain the condition of your property according to the housing health and safety standards of your area.
- Evict any bad tenants who don't pay rent on time or break the terms of your rental agreement.

You should insist on having the power of choosing to handle any of the above issues if you think you can do a better and cheaper job. For example, you can request that all repairs be made by a certain licensed contractor you trust and who charges you less.

How to Choose the Perfect Manager
for Your Rental Property

To hire the right property manager, you need to first ensure that your manager is licensed and certified. Most countries issue licenses in property management and hiring a licensed manager ensures that he has at least gone through some basic training in real estate management. For example, if you own rental properties in the USA, you can visit the Institute of Real Estate Management web site (**www.irem.org**) and search function to find your real estate ideal property managers.

The next step is to interview your property manager before you hire him. Always ask for references and feedback from current and past clients so you can contact them directly to ask about the manager's performance.

If you're making use of a real estate management company, insist they assign the same permanent employee to manage your properties. This way, he'll be more familiar with your property and your tenants.

An important point is whether the companies you approach are purely in the property management business, or real estate brokers who also happen to dabble in real estate management.

Real estate brokers who offer real estate management services as a sideline may be cheaper, but they may also lack the specialized skills to run your property smoothly. Be extra careful if you're considering hiring them as your real estate property managers.

Source: **http://www.propertydo.com**.

Tips for Real Estate Investors

Real estate investing is not a one-size-fits-all process. As a result, it makes the most sense to approach investing by determining your personal needs and goals first, then applying the appropriate strategies. This will allow you to focus and reach your goals more quickly and with the least amount of risk.

The most popular investment strategy in real estate is what we call "buy and hold," often called "landlording" or investing in rental properties. The plan is to buy a property, rent it out to tenants and then hold onto it for some period of time. You ultimately make money from the cash flow generated by the property, the pay-down of the debt and any increase in value the property appreciates while you own it.

It sounds so simple that many people with very little investment knowledge go out and buy a property, thinking it's easy. Many new investors do this even though they have limited capital to invest, and don't have cash reserves to weather any financial storms. They jump in and buy the property using all their money. Soon after, they realize it's not as easy as it looks—vacancies, unplanned repairs and other expenses begin to mount, and suddenly the investor is under water and has no money to keep up with the costs. Regrettably, they then turn into motivated sellers, and dump the property below market value just to stop the hurtful cash drain. What's the problem here? It's that the investor chose the wrong investment strategy for them at the time.

Three Types of Cash in Investing

There are three types of cash that form a part of your investment goals: cash today, cash tomorrow and cash to play. Think of them as the combination that can unlock the vault of long-term wealth. They identify what kind of cash you really need right now, and help you set a course for long-term success.

1. Cash Today

This is the most important type of cash to think about. Cash today is the income and/or capital you need to fund your current living needs, such as mortgage payments, food, taxes and other bills you are required to pay. Most people satisfy their cash today needs by having a job. However, when it comes to real estate, there are certain strategies you can employ to help increase the amount of cash today you acquire.

A lot of people fall in love with the concept of what is called "passive income." They chase investment situations that are all about future cash flow streams, but they ignore their cash today needs. As a result, they end up investing in the wrong kinds of properties, for the wrong reasons. They usually end up cash starved and have to sell their investments in a panic, usually at a loss. They are investment rich, but cash poor, and that path leads to the burial ground where you find many motivated sellers. You must satisfy your cash today needs before you worry about trying to create cash tomorrow or cash to play.

2. Cash Tomorrow

This is making decisions and taking actions today that generate you a stream of income tomorrow, or more accurately, sometime in the future. Cash tomorrow is also referred to as "leveraged income" because other people's time, money and energy are used to build and achieve our own goals. Focusing on your cash tomorrow needs means investing on the basis that you may not generate any cash or cash flow immediately, but that there will be a stream of income to you in the very near future. Also, that stream of income may increase or decrease over time, depending on the strategy you employ. Your goal is to eventually replace the active income you currently earn (i.e., income from a job or small business you operate).

The secret to wealth is building your cash tomorrow income streams to pay for the lifestyle you want in the future. Cash tomorrow investing strategies are vehicles that allow you to create income streams without having to keep making new deals, month after month. Cash tomorrow investing Is all about converting the cash you have now into positive cash flow stream that continues to benefit you for years to come.

3. Cash to Play

Cash to play is the planning and process involved with converting the results of your cash today and cash tomorrow investing into a cash or cash flow situation that supports your "retirement" lifestyle. Retirement is defined as a point in time, no matter your age, when you no longer work or actively invest because you have to, and where you are financially secure enough to enjoy what you desire most in your life.

Cash to play is when you position your investments in such a way that they support your goals and dreams, when you decide you no longer want to actively manage your investments. It's the end game of what you do with the investments (and results) that you've created in your cash today and cash tomorrow investments. It's about taking what you've created, and building a plan that allows you to enjoy those things you love to do.

Source: Greg Habstritt, founder of **SimpleWealth.com**

TED'S TIPS

- Understand the difference between lifestyle, investment and hybrid properties.

- Be sure to fully research the area you wish to buy in *before* making an offer.

- When buying a property for lifestyle purposes, be sure that it and its surrounding area has most, if not all, of the amenities that you want near a home.

- When buying an investment property, consider the amount of rent you will receive in order to get the best cash flow. Also consider how much it will appreciate, and compare that to other areas of the same town or city.

- Don't let emotions get into the way of your purchasing decision. Stick to the plan.

- Do your homework when choosing a property manager, including how to choose a good company and what services they offer. Also be clear on the fees, as that will impact your cash flow from the property.

- Many homeowners associations do not allow rentals (you must obtain such verification in writing). Amendments to condo rules and regulations are much easier to do in the US, i.e., you do not necessarily need to file such amendments at land titles and a barebones majority will usually suffice. Therefore amendments are much more fickle. Two things you need to do 1) get permission to rent in writing and 2) ask for it to be grandfathered in so that if it ever changes you have that permission in writing.

9

Of Offers and Counter-offers

· **On a Saturday in** late June, Nancy waved at Ted, who was cutting the lawn with a push mower in the back yard of their Vancouver home.

"Ted, I need to talk to you. It's urgent," Nancy called. "What is it?" Ted yelled back. "Can't it wait until I'm done?" "No, I think you'll want to talk about this now." Ted doffed his baseball cap and left it on the handle of the mower. "Sam just called. She said there's a unit for sale in that building we like so much in Phoenix. It's in our price range. She wants to know if we're interested."

"Wow, that was sudden! For some reason, I didn't expect to hear from her for months. We were pretty picky about what we wanted," he said.

"I know, but she is about to email the pictures and I think we should go and take a look on the computer right now. I didn't think you'd want to wait," Nancy said.

"No, let's go," he said.

They rushed inside. Ted sat in the chair in front of the computer and Nancy stood hovering over him as he opened the email from Sam.

"Hello Ted and Nancy," Sam wrote. "As I just told Nancy on the phone, I am pleased to report that a unit in that building you admired in Phoenix has just come up for sale. The owner has taken a job overseas and is interested in selling as soon as possible. The price also reflects their desire for a quick sale. Here are a few pictures of the inside of the unit. I think it might be perfectly suited to your investment needs. Let me know what you think!"

Ted and Nancy scanned the photos. Nancy commented on how much natural light there was in the suite, and Ted liked the living space and large-sized bedrooms.

"I think this might be our baby," Ted said. "What do you think?"

"I think you might be right. What should we do now?"

"Well, we've already seen the building once, and I've stayed in the city twice. We've researched what we want to buy, and why. I say we're ready to put down a deposit," Ted said.

"Shouldn't we go look at it?"

Ted paused and thought to himself: "What would Sid suggest?"

"What would Sid suggest?" Nancy asked out loud.

"Well, I don't know what he would say, but I think one of us should go. It can be you this time if you want, or I can go." Ted said.

Nancy thought about it for a moment. "As much as I'd like to go, I have a big project at work that I can't get away from. Why don't you go? You still have some vacation time left. Maybe Sid would be interested in going with you."

"I don't need Sid for this. I think he's helped enough. Besides, it's already 30 degrees in Toronto right now. Why would he want to visit Phoenix where it's even warmer? I think I want to do this on our own. Okay?"

"Sure," Nancy said. "How exciting! Give Sam a call and let her know we're interested and that you're coming down to take a look."

"I should also probably be able to find a cheap flight this time of year, and maybe this time I'll take a direct route, which I didn't realize they had the last time I went in the fall," Ted said.

"We're so smart now, don't you think?" Nancy said. "It just feels right this time."

IT'S THE ONE

Ted stepped off the plane in Phoenix, where Sam was waiting for him in the arrivals area. She walked up to Ted and extended her hand. Ted gave her a hug instead.

"Where I'm from, we like to hug, especially when we're appreciative," Ted said.

"Oh, okay," Sam said, taken aback. "Where I'm from, we don't even hug at funerals, but that's okay. I think your people might have it right."

She walked Ted to her car, and they drove straight to the townhome complex where the property was waiting to be shown.

"So, this isn't a foreclosure, right?" Ted asked. "Just a unit that came up for sale. No issues, no special conditions?"

"No, nothing like that. It's just a couple who are moving overseas and they want to sell, soon. They're moving to Dubai."

"Dubai?" Ted asked, surprised. "It wasn't hot enough for them here in Phoenix?"

"I guess not," Sam said with a chuckle.

As she pulled up to the complex, Ted remembered how well kept it was. It looked exactly the same as he remembered, and that was a good thing.

"My wife has sent me with a bunch of questions," Ted said, then pulled out a folded up paper from his shirt pocket. "I'll keep it close by."

"She's a smart cookie, that Nancy," Sam said.

"She is, and we couldn't have gotten to this point without her pushing for us to do our homework and really think about what we should buy," Ted said.

"Well, it sounds like the two of you have really thought hard about this," Sam said. "And the fact that she trusts you to come see this without her shows a real level of trust. That's a good marriage."

Ted nodded. "Well, she sent me with a video camera and I have to email her the video before I sign anything or . . . What did she say again? Oh right, or she'll kill me!"

Sam laughed as she pulled the car into a visitor parking space. Ted shook his head.

"No, it's true, we're a good team, Nancy and me," Ted said, as he unhooked his seatbelt and stepped out of the car. "I've known her since I was 18 years old, but I was too chicken to ask her on a date until I was 30. She said no."

Sam was still laughing as she stepped out of the car, grabbing her briefcase and locking the door.

"So when did she finally say 'yes'?" Sam asked.

"Well, she didn't. It took another couple years and finally she asked me out!" Ted said as he recalled the story. "That's sweet," said Sam. "Nice story."

The two walked towards the unit and Sam unlocked the door. Before she turned the handle she turned to Ted and said, "Ready?"

"More than ever," he said. "Show me my future invest-ment, please!"

Sam pushed open the door and allowed Ted to step in first. The unit was on two levels, had two bedrooms, including a huge master suite upstairs, as well as two bathrooms with new slab granite counters.

"As the listing I sent you and Nancy stated, this building isn't new, but has been completely renovated from top to bottom," Sam said as she walked Ted through.

"According to the seller's agent, the inside was renovated less than a year ago. New kitchen and bathroom."

"It's really quite nice, isn't it?" Ted said.

"I think it is, but it's your decision, Ted. I am not going to talk you into it. I just know that you and Nancy really liked the other units you saw in here last time you were down. Frankly, I think this one is even nicer than either of those."

"I agree," said Ted. "The asking price again is $169,000; is that right?"

"Yes, $168,900 actually," Sam said. "I recommend we start by putting in an offer for $150,000, and see what they say. I don't know that you'll get it for that much less, but we should try."

"Well, actually I don't want to negotiate in round numbers; my buddy Sid says that's a mistake. He uses obscure numbers and he says the counter-offers always come back in bigger round numbers. Let's start with $149,986, okay?"

"Okay, Ted, you're the boss," Sam replied.

Ted then pulled out the video camera Nancy sent with him and started taping the unit to download and send her later. He walked through the house with Sam, as she described into the camera for Nancy all the features of the unit. Then they took shots from outside, including the two-car garage and the pool, which was shared by all of the residents.

Ted then turned the camera lens towards his face. "Nancy, sweetie, I really like it. I hope you will, too."

He then shut off the camera. "Can I send it to her from your office?" he asked Sam.

"Sure, no problem. Meantime, I've got three names of home inspectors for you. You might want to give them a call and see if they're available in the next few days, in case you need them. How long are you here again?" Sam asked.

"I'm here until Sunday. I had to take three days off work. I think my boss is starting to wonder what I'm really up to!" Ted said. "Luckily I've got some extra vacation days from last year."

"Great, that means you can take your time. I should also warn you that closing the deal may not happen as quickly as you might be used to in Canada," Sam said. "The banks are pretty swamped here. Have you seen a bank yet to talk about financing? I'm not trying to push you into this Ted, but just want to help smooth out the process if Nancy does give it the thumbs up."

"The bank is next on my list. I'm seeing them first thing tomorrow," Ted said. "Got an appointment at 10."

They arrived at Sam's office and she recruited a young computer-savvy colleague to help Ted download the video into a computer and email it to Nancy. A few minutes later, Ted called her on his cell phone.

"Honey? It's there. The video. Check it out and call me back."

He then hung up and sat with Sam in her office.

"So, how's your husband? How's the basketball business?" Ted said, fishing.

"Oh! That reminds me," Sam said. She then opened her desk drawer and pulled out an envelope and handed it to Ted.

"It's a couple seats for Friday's baseball game—the Arizona Diamondbacks at Chase Field. I assume you like baseball?"

Ted's eyes lit up. "Yes, I love it! Thanks!"

"My pleasure," said Sam.

Seconds later, Ted's phone rang. It was Nancy.

"Uh huh. Yes. Yes, I asked that," Ted said in response to questions on the other end of the line. "Yes, she said that was the case. Yes. Yes."

There was a long pause.

"Okay. Are you sure? Yes, I'll be sure to do that. Yes. Okay. I'll call you later. Oh, sweetie. I love you!"

Ted hung up the phone. "She said no."

Sam looked surprised.

"Just kidding. Let's make an offer!" Ted said.

Sam smiled and shook Ted's hand. "We could hug?" she said.

"Okay," Ted said and jumped up and gave Sam a quick embrace.

"Now," Sam said, again serious. "Let's draw up that offer."

ADVICE FROM THE MORTGAGE BROKER

Ted sat down across the desk from Darlene, a mortgage broker in Phoenix, and told her he was there to follow up on a mortgage pre-approval application. Nancy had already faxed her the paperwork and Ted was now there in person, since he was making the offer.

"We put in an offer last night and they countered this morning. We put in another offer about an hour ago. Meanwhile, I wanted to get approved for a mortgage. I think we might make a deal later today," Ted said.

Darlene pulled their file, which included the documents they needed to get the loan, such as proof of his and Nancy's employment history, their credit history as well bank statements and a copy of their passports.

"My wife threw in a few extra things there she thought you might like to see, I told her it was probably too much, but . . ."

"It looks great," Darlene said. "More than enough is better than not enough. Looks like you and your wife did your homework. You would be surprised at the number of people who don't."

Ted felt proud. He then explained that, while the house was selling for $168,900, they were hoping to get it for less. They already had them down to $160,000. He said the plan was to buy a house worth no more than $160,000, and put 50 per cent down in cash from savings and after taking equity out of their Vancouver home. The other 50 per cent they wanted to finance with a US mortgage.

As Ted talked, Darlene clicked away on her computer, putting together some calculations.

"Let's get you approved for something at your maximum, and then if you pay less that will just be extra money you can use to renovate or anything else you might need," Darlene said.

She then tapped away on her calculator, using Ted's example of 50 per cent down on $160,000.

"Based on a 25-year mortgage of $80,000, at an interest rate of 5 per cent, your monthly payments will be approximately $468," Darlene concluded.

Ted nodded. "That sounds good. Like I said, I think it will be less than that, but let's see what they come back with."

Ted wrote down his cell phone number and thanked Darlene for her help. He promised to get back to her as soon as the deal was made.

Getting Financing in the US

As a foreign national, there are different mortgage financing options available to you. The terms of the loan are bit more favorable if you are seeking to purchase a second (vacation) home in the United States. The definition of a vacation home is that you intend to use it for recreational purposes during a portion of the year and you do not derive any monetary benefits from ownership, meaning you will not rent the place to a tenant. You will be asked to sign a disclosure statement to this effect.

If you're purchasing a vacation home, you will need a minimum of 30% down. So, for a $200,000 purchase, the required down payment is $60,000. Additionally, you will need to demonstrate that you have between three and six months of liquid reserves. This is calculated by multiplying your monthly payment by a factor of three to six. Not all lenders require this reserve, but many do, so if you have it, the better it is for you.

As part of the approval process, you will be asked to show two to three months of bank statements demonstrating that the funds for a down payment and reserves are available. The lender is very suspicious when there are large depositions in your account (beyond your regular income), so be prepared to explain if that's the case. Finally, the assets need to be in a Canadian bank and the mortgage lender will request verification directly from your bank.

You will need to show a copy of your Canadian passport and/or driver's license. Some lenders may request only one of these two, but be prepared to furnish both if requested.

If you intend to purchase an investment property in the United States, then the terms are somewhat more stringent. You will be required to put more than 30% down (determined on a case-by-case basis), as well as demonstrate more reserves (possibly up to 12 months). All other aspects of the loan are the same.

If you feel like these are conditions you can fulfill, the first step is to complete a mortgage application with a reputable lender. You will be asked information about such things as your employment and income and available liquid assets. In subsequent steps, you will be required to furnish a letter of employment, relevant bank statements and a copy of the passport (or driver's license). Once all the information has been verified, the lender can then make a credit decision.

You may not need a particular property in mind to go through this process. Some mortgage brokers can do what is called a "credit approval" for you up to a certain price range. Then, as long as the property you end up purchasing is within that price range, all they need is an approval on the property/appraisal. After that they are able to close the transaction.

Finally, as you are aware, US credit markets have been in a state of flux. This means loan programs have been changing more often than in the past. While these loan features are currently available, there is no assurance that these terms and conditions will remain in the future.

Source: The Phoenix Real Estate Guy, **www.phoenixreales tateguy.com**.

As he walked out of Darlene's office building, Ted's phone rang. It was Sam.

"Are you sitting down, Ted?" Sam said.

"No, I'm walking out of the bank. Should I be sitting?" he asked.

"Your buddy's pricing strategy is different, I must say, but it works. They accepted the offer at $158,465. It's conditional on financing and home inspection, of course. But assuming it all goes well, you'll be a US homeowner. How does it feel?"

Ted was silent for a second.

"Ted?" Sam said. "Are you okay?"

He sighed. "I'm excellent, Sam. Thanks. I can't wait to call Nancy. We did it!"

"I assume she'll be very happy," Sam said.

"The first thing she'll tell me to do is get a home inspection," Ted said. "She'll be happy, but she'll be cautiously optimistic. That's just Nancy."

Ted hung up the phone and called his wife. The conversation went almost exactly as he predicted.

"Guess what? The counter-offer is accepted at $158,465," Ted said.

"I knew they would! Sid was right." Nancy shouted on the other end of the line. "That's great. When's the home inspection?"

"I knew you'd ask me that!" Ted said. "Well, I already called two of the three references Sam gave us, and one of them is available tomorrow afternoon. I said I would get back to him today."

"Call him now!" "I'll hang up. Call me later. And sweetie, just one more thing I wanted to say for now . . . Good work! I'm so proud of you." Nancy exlaimed.

Ted felt proud of himself, too. But his work wasn't done yet. First he had to attend to the home inspection. Then he had to get confirmation of the financing. Assuming all went well, there was the closing, which Sam said would be in 60 days. He hadn't crossed the finish line just yet.

THE HOME INSPECTION

At 1:30 the next afternoon, Ted and Sam met Dirk, the home inspector, outside the complex where Ted's new unit was waiting to be prodded.

"I know this complex," Dirk said. "I did an inspection here a couple months back. Nice spot."

"Thanks," Ted said. "How was it back then? Good shape?"

"Well, it looks good from the outside, doesn't it?" Dirk said. "But let's reserve judgment until I give it the full treatment."

"Good thinking," Ted said. Sam agreed. They both followed Dirk into the suite. Sam and Ted sat at the kitchen table while Dirk explained how the home inspection would work.

Home Inspection FAQs

What is an Inspection?

An inspection is a visual examination of the structure and systems of a building. If you're thinking of buying a home, condominium, mobile home or commercial building, you should have it thoroughly inspected before the final purchase by an experienced and impartial professional inspector.

What Does an Inspection Include?

A complete inspection includes a visual examination of the building from top to bottom. The inspector evaluates and reports the condition of the structure, roof, foundation, drainage, plumbing, heating system, central air-conditioning system, visible insulation, walls, windows and doors. Only those items that are visible and accessible by normal means are included in the report.

When Do I Request an Inspector?

The best time to consult the inspector is right after you've made an offer on your new building. The real estate contract usually allows for a grace period to inspect the building. Ask your agent to include this inspection clause in the contract, making your purchase obligation contingent on the findings of a professional inspection.

Can a Building "FAIL" the Inspection?

No. A professional inspection is simply an examination into the current condition of your prospective real estate purchase. It's not an appraisal or a Municipal Code inspection. An inspector, therefore, will not pass or fail a building, but will simply describe its condition and indicate which items are in need of minor or major repair or replacement.

What if the Report Reveals Problems?

If the inspector finds problems in a building, it does not necessarily mean you shouldn't buy It, only that you will know in advance what type of repairs to anticipate. A seller may be willing to make repairs because of significant problems discovered by the inspector. If your budget is tight, or if you don't wish to become involved in future repair work, you may decide that this is not the property for you. The choice is yours.

If the Report is Favorable, Did I Really Need an Inspection?

Definitely! Now you can complete your purchase with peace of mind about the condition of the property and its equipment and systems. You may have learned a few things about your property from the inspection report and will want to keep that information for your future reference. Above all, you can rest assured that you're making a well-informed purchase decision and that you'll be able to enjoy or occupy your new home or building the way you want.

Why Do I Need an Inspection?

The purchase of a home or commercial building is one of the largest single investments you will ever make. You should know exactly what to expect—both indoors and out—in terms of needed and future repairs and maintenance. A fresh coat of paint could be hiding serious structural problems. Stains on the ceiling may indicate a chronic roof leakage problem or may be simply the result of a single incident. The inspector interprets these and other clues, and then presents a professional opinion as to the condition of the property so you can avoid unpleasant surprises afterward. Of course, an inspection will also point out the positive aspects of a building, as well as the type of maintenance needed to keep it in good shape. After the inspection, you will have a much clearer understanding of the property you are about to purchase, and be able to make your decision with confidence.

As a seller, if you have owned your building for a period of time, an inspection can identify potential problems in the sale of your building and can recommend preventive measures, which might avoid future expensive repairs.

Can I Inspect the Building Myself?

Even the most experienced homeowner lacks the knowledge and expertise of a professional inspector who has inspected hundreds, and perhaps thousands, of homes and buildings in their career. An inspector is equally familiar with the critical elements of construction and with the proper installation, maintenance and inter-relationships of these elements. Above all, most buyers find it difficult to remain completely objective and unemotional about the building they really want, and this may lead to a poor assessment.

What Will the Inspection Cost?

The inspection fee for a typical single-family house or commercial building varies geographically, as does the cost of housing. Similarly, within a geographic area, inspection fees charged by different inspection services may vary depending upon the size or features of the building, age and type of structure. However, the cost should not be a factor in the decision whether to have a physical inspection. You might save many times the cost of the inspection if you are able to have the seller perform repairs based on significant problems revealed by the inspector. Consult your professional agent for guidance.

Should I Attend the Inspection?

It is not necessary for you to be present for the inspection, but it is a good idea. By following the inspector through the inspection, observing and asking questions, you will learn about the new building and get some tips on general maintenance. This information will be of great help to you after you've moved in.

Source: California Real Estate Inspection Association, **http://www.creia.org/i4a/pages/index.cfm?pageid=3321# Inspection**.

Other Home Inspection Tips

- Houses built before 1978 may contain lead paint. This may be a concern, especially if you have children.
- Roof repair is one of the costliest repair jobs. To this end, try to determine the remaining life of the roof.
- Ventilation in the attic area is important. Better ventilation means longer life of your roof.
- Make sure that the property is not in any areas subject to flooding and that inclination of the land does not cause wet foundation problems. You can visually determine this by looking at the elevation of the soil around the property.
- Homes built in the 1960s and 1970s may have aluminum wires. Aluminum wires may cause fire due to overheating. They should be replaced by a licensed electrician. How can you differentiate the types of wires? Aluminum wires are silver-white in color, while copper wires are reddish.

- Old homes may have lead or galvanized steel water pipes. They need to be replaced for health reasons. Lead is a well-known poison, especially for children.
- Some furnaces, especially those horizontal ones placed in the attic have caused fires in the past. There is a long list of such furnaces that have been recalled. They should be replaced.
- Earth-wood contact causes rot and insect penetration. You need to periodically check the status of such locations to avoid insect or termite infestation. You can observe termite infestation if the wood material has surface damage but you cannot see such damage if it's inside.

Source: **http://www.buyinghome.org/foreclosure_inspection_tips.htm.**

"I'm not sure if you've been through one of these before," Dirk began.

"I have a house back home in Vancouver," Ted said, "but I've never been through an inspection of a building that's part of a complex. I assume you check some of the common areas as well?"

"I do. It's a good idea to know what kind of maintenance the common areas might need, such as the patios and the pool, which I see you have one of here," Dirk said. "Some people don't think condos and townhomes need inspections, but I think that's a mistake. Of course, I'm biased, but you'd be shocked at some of the problems these buildings have that nobody looks into before they buy."

"That reminds me," Sam said. "I will also have the homeowner's association governing documents for you later today. They promised to fax them over to my office by the end of the day."

"What do they tell me, again?" Ted asked.

"That's where you find out about any issues the building might have; they are discussed in the minutes by the committee that oversees the care of the building. Do you know what I mean?"

"Yes, I think so," Ted said. "In Vancouver, they're called strata corporations, and I think in other provinces they are the condo corporations. Each building has one, a president, a secretary and other board members. I have a friend who's the president of his strata back home. They had to deal with a leaky condo issue there a number of years back. What a mess that was."

"I remember hearing about that," Sam said. "I have a friend who used to live in Vancouver and she told me all about it. Scary stuff. Well, the minutes will give you some history of this building. I've sold a few in here in recent months and I don't recall that there are any issues, but let's see what they come back with. Meantime, Dirk here is going to give us his professional opinion on what he sees. Aren't you, Dirk?"

"Yup," Dirk said, as he wrapped a tool belt around his waist and held a flashlight in his right hand. "Let's get started."

As he moved through the unit, Dirk explained what he was checking for, including the foundation, interior and exterior and all electric and mechanical parts of the home. He checked the heating and air conditioning systems, the electrical, plumbing and fixtures, even the garage door opener. As Dirk worked, Sam showed Ted a pile of receipts on the kitchen counter left behind by the owners, including warranties and service records for the appliances and heating and air conditioning as well as the gas fireplace and the alarm system. They also left behind some utility bills to show the cost of electricity and the heat and air conditioning.

"Looks like they laid it out here for you," Sam said. "That's what you want to see in a seller. Proof they took care of the place."

Ted was getting excited. He could hardly wait for Dirk to finish the job of inspecting the home. "How much longer do you think?" Ted said to Dirk, like a kid in the back seat of a car on a long trip.

"Not long now," Dirk said. "Just want to check a couple more things. If you want to have a seat I can give you my assessment in about five minutes."

Ted went and sat in the dining room, tapping his fingers on the table.

Sam sat beside him. "Let's hope it's all good news," she said.

Dirk then came into the room with his report.

"Overall, I have to say the place is in pretty good shape. The air conditioning system needs a new filter and some of the faucets need new washers," Dirk said.

He went on to list a few other "minor" items. While Dirk called them "issues," none of it sounded bad to Ted at all. In fact, his own house had a lot more problems than Dirk was mentioning in this list.

"What do you think Dirk? Does it pass?" Ted asked.

Dirk looked up at Ted and said: "I'd say you've got yourself a well-maintained place here. You might want to ask them to fix some of the small stuff on this list before they sell it to you. But of all the places I look at on a regular basis, this one is definitely a pass."

"Yes!" Ted said, and jumped off his chair.

"Now, that's a happy buyer," Sam said.

Dirk handed Ted his own workbook listing the results of the inspection and Ted handed Dirk a check. Dirk then shook both Sam and Ted's hands, picked up his toolbox and brief-case and walked back to his truck.

Ted turned to Sam and smiled. "It's all coming together nicely."

"Did you get the financing approved?" Sam said.

"Yup," Ted said. "Nancy already sent in the paperwork and the bank called me this morning. It's approved. And I have a termite inspector coming by in about a half hour."

"Great!" said Sam. "How about I buy you a coffee at the café downstairs and we wait for the termite man to show up?"

Ted followed Sam to the café.

A DONE DEAL

The next morning, after the house got the all clear from the termite inspector and Ted learned there were no issues in the homeowner association minutes, he met Sam at her office to sign the documents. Sam then faxed a copy to Nancy at work. She signed them and immediately faxed them back.

Sam, with Ted seated across from her, called Nancy at her Vancouver office and put her on speakerphone.

"Are you there," Sam said into the phone.

"I'm here!" Nancy said. "How's Ted doing?"

"He looks a little pale right now," Sam responded. "But I have to say, Nancy, I think he did better than you thought he would."

Ted looked puzzled at Sam. "Hey, what have you two been discussing while I wasn't around?"

Sam and Nancy laughed together.

"Nothing, sweetie," Nancy said through the speakerphone. "We're just teasing."

"He asked a lot of good questions, Nancy. He played some serious hardball with the sellers too. You should be proud," Sam said.

"I am," Nancy said. "Ted, honey, we're investment property owners. How do you feel?"

Ted felt a lump in his throat. The reality suddenly hit home. "I think I feel a bit nauseous," Ted said.

"Don't get buyer's remorse on me now, Ted!" Nancy shouted through the phone. "We've been through way too much for you to go that way on me!"

"I'm fine, Nancy," Ted said. "I think it's just the heat."

Sam then explained how the rest of the process worked. She said the deal would close in 60 days, and that if they wanted to rent out the unit she could recommend a few property management firms.

"Congratulations!" Sam said to Ted and Nancy. "Welcome to homeownership in Phoenix."

Top Real Estate Negotiation Tips

Always know your bottom and upper limits that you are prepared to pay or sell at. Write them down on a piece of paper and stick to them.

When bidding or selling, always move in small steps on the price and in odd numbers. Never move in round numbers as you say to the other side you are prepared to move. For example, if the asking price is $275,000, the seller will move down $10,000, you move up $758 and it looks like you're really tight in your price.

In an actual negotiation, always remember to breathe, as you need 35% more oxygen to help you think. Fill your tummy like a balloon on counts of four, hold for eight seconds and release for four. Do this 10 times in sets of three prior to your negotiation, and it will have you feeling nice and calm and give you the ability to think.

Never fall for the time trap, take time out in a negotiation, leave the room and call back on the phone. A seller rushing you means they are happy with the price they want you to pay.

1. Always look at the bigger picture. If somebody will not move on price, get them to leave selected furniture, garden pieces or whatever will add value.
2. Run down what you buy and talk up what you sell.
3. Research your investment and take time to prepare for your negotiation. Quick purchases usually lead to greater pain and regret.
4. Be respectful to the people you're negotiating with; help them make the right decision. Remember, it's a big decision for them as well.
5. Practice your negotiation. Role play it with a family member or colleague and get them to play the opposite party.
6. Negotiations are one of the most important life skills you will have, or in 90% of the population's case, will not have.
7. Never, ever gloat when you nail the deal as this has a funny way of coming back to bite you.

A challenge: If you want to really improve your negotiations skills, I challenge you to ask for a discount on every item you purchase that is more than $50. I mean everywhere. They can say no or yes, but you are getting a free education and you'll save lots of money.

Source: Robert McKernan, McKernan Training Solutions, Ireland.

TED'S TIPS

- When looking at the home you may want to buy, look for potential issues behind large pictures on the wall and under rugs or furniture on the floor.

- Look for stains on the ceiling or carpets that might indicate water damage.

- Check all appliances to confirm they work, including the stove burners, oven, garbage disposal, dishwasher, washer and dryer, and the water heater.

- Run water in all sinks and tubs, and flush the toilets to make sure they drain properly. If the landscaping includes an irrigation system, check to see that it works.

- Drive around the neighborhood and observe the condition of the homes. Are lawns mowed? Are there old cars rusting in driveways? Ask neighbors how they like living in the area. Is this really where you want to live or invest?

- Hire a home inspector. It's worth the money to hire a professional who works in the area to look at the home and understand what the potential issues might be.

- Also hire separate professionals to look for termites and other pests.

- Read the seller's property disclosure report and check every item on it.

- Ask to see receipts for repairs to the home.

- Read the purchase contract carefully to determine if there are any deadlines for challenging the seller's disclosure report or for having your own inspections conducted.

- Make sure the building allows rentals. Some associations have restrictions or prohibit them altogether.

- Read the deed restrictions, also called CC&Rs (covenants, conditions and restrictions). You might find some of the CC&Rs are very strict, especially those addressing landscaping, RV parking, play equipment, satellite antennas, and other common amenities—particularly if the subdivision is governed by a homeowner's association.

- If you are buying a unit in a multi-family building, get a copy of the homeowner's association minutes from as far back as possible to ensure there were no issues, past or present, that may lead to costly repairs down the road.

10

Of Escrow Officers and Closing the Deal

Nancy pulled up in the car to the arrivals level area outside the Vancouver International Airport and saw Ted standing outside on the sidewalk, waiting. She honked twice to get his attention. He waved and hopped into the car, throwing his bag in the back seat.

"Welcome home, new homeowner," Nancy said, and gave him a kiss.

"It's good to be back," Ted said. "What a trip!"

"You did well," Nancy said. She then pulled away from the curb and drove through the busy Sunday traffic back to their house.

After stepping through the front door and into the dining room, Ted noticed a number of documents strewn across the table.

"What's this?" he asked.

"We've got a lot to take care of before we officially take ownership. I thought I'd help us get started," Nancy.

Ted looked quickly over the documents. They included information on an escrow agent, title insurance, home insurance and documents from their Canadian-based bank to take equity out of their current home.

"I have been doing a lot of reading since you left, assuming we'd make the deal. I've learned all about escrow, title insurance and I've got some information on hiring a property manager."

"Tell me about escrow," Ted said. "Sam talked about it, but I have to be honest, I didn't fully understand."

"Remember when we closed our home here in Vancouver?" Nancy asked. Ted nodded.

"We used a real estate lawyer, right?" Nancy continued. "Well, in the US, you can use an escrow agent. Basically, what they do is handle the closing. They can also handle the title insurance. They make sure we get the mortgage, that the transaction costs are paid, that the seller's mortgage is paid off, and that the seller gets their money."

"And title insurance, we have that here, right, and we need it in the US, too, of course?" Ted said.

"Yes, that's right. The title company—which in the US is usually associated with the escrow agent—examines the chain of titles from previous owners and makes sure there are no problems such as liens due to unpaid taxes or stuff like that. If we buy the house, we are vulnerable to such claims on the property. Title insurance protects us from that."

"We also have to get home insurance in place before the closing," Ted added.

"Yes, I have a few quotes already. Take a look," Nancy said, and handed Ted three sheets of paper from the right side of the table.

Ted glanced at the quotes and then put down the papers.

"I think I am going to deal with this later. I just walked in the door. How about we get a couple beers, barbeque some steaks and celebrate tonight. When will Susie be home from soccer?" Ted asked.

"Not until later; she's staying at her friend's house afterwards for supper," Nancy said.

"You get the beer and I'll start up the barbeque," Nancy said and left the room.

Ted looked down again at the real estate papers on the table. He felt relieved—and confident. At this time last year, he couldn't even pronounce escrow, and now he was in it! What a difference time and a little education makes, he thought.

Ted felt an urge to call Sid. He grabbed the phone and dialed Sid's home number in Toronto.

"Hello," Sid answered.

"Sid! It's Ted. Guess what?" Ted said.

"You didn't? You bought a home, didn't you?" Sid said.

"Yup, we bought it a couple days ago. A townhouse in Phoenix. Good rental area, got it for $158,465—which was about $10,000 below asking. We're really happy with it."

"Ted, that's great. Congratulations!" Sid said.

"I bet you already knew, didn't you?" Ted said.

"No, I had no idea," Sid replied. "I mean, I knew you went on that trip a few weeks ago to look at some places, but I had no idea you were ready to buy. That's great!"

"Sid, I wanted to buy a year ago but it wasn't until now that I was truly ready." "Hey, are you telling me that you and Nancy haven't discussed it already?"

"No, we haven't," Sid answered. "Seriously, Ted. I haven't spoken to Nancy since the last time I called there and she answered the phone, last month."

Ted felt even more proud. Nancy didn't turn to Sid, as she had in the past, for advice on whether they were doing the right thing. They did it on their own.

"Sid, I can't thank you enough for all of the advice you gave Nancy and me in this process. And for talking me into that first trip to Phoenix last fall. You saved my butt, again," Ted said.

"I really didn't do anything," Sid said. "I just helped put you on the right path, but you made the journey all on your own, you and Nancy. Congratulations."

"Thanks, Sid. It feels good." "Nancy and I are about to make supper, but I just wanted to give you a quick call. You're still coming next month with the family, right?"

"You betcha. We're looking forward to it." "'Bye for now."

Ted hung up the phone, grabbed two beers from the fridge, and met Nancy on the deck outside.

What You Need to Know about Closing

Closing (or settlement as it is known in some parts of the US) is the final step in executing a real estate transaction.

The closing date is set during the negotiation phase, and is usually several weeks after the offer is formally accepted. On the closing date, the parties consummate the purchase contract, and ownership of the property is transferred to the buyer. In most jurisdictions, ownership is officially transferred when the contract is registered at the cadastre, or in most US states, the office of the County Recorder of the county in which the property is located.

Several things happen during closing:

- The buyer (or his bank) delivers a check (generally, in the US, a cashier's check or wire transfer) for the balance owed on the purchase price.
- The seller signs the deed over to the buyer and hands over the keys.
- A title company, lawyer or civil law notary registers the new deed with the local land registry office.
- The seller receives a check for the proceeds of the sale, less closing costs and mortgage payouts.

Closing in escrow usually occurs in the western half of the US states. A title company (rather than a lawyer) or other trusted party holds the money and the signed deed, and arranges for the transfer. This is primarily so the seller can give up ownership of the property, and the buyer can hand over the payment, without both parties having to be present at the same time. Escrow ensures an orderly transaction, or if something goes wrong, an orderly termination of the agreement.

On the eastern side of the US, settlement (as closing is called) takes place on a specified date and time during which all parties (usually including the agents involved) meet at a settlement company presided over or supervised by a lawyer or settlement agent. At which time, the settlement agent disburses all funds listed on the settlement statement (in form of certified or wired funds) and the property takes place, and the deed is then recorded by the company.

Source: **www.wikipedia.org**.

What You Need to Know about Escrow

How Does an Escrow Work?

The principals to the escrow, or agents, will provide the escrow officer with a copy of the purchase contract, deposit and any necessary information for the escrow officer to prepare escrow instructions or supplemental escrow instructions. These instructions reiterate the specific requirements that have been agreed upon in order to close. Upon review and execution by both buyer and seller, the escrow holder will proceed in accordance with the escrow instructions. When all conditions of the escrow are met, the escrow holder will then have all necessary documents recorded and close the escrow. As escrow is a neutral third party, the escrow holder can operate only on written instructions. Therefore, it is important to be concise in instructing the agent and/or escrow holder.

Who Chooses an Escrow and When?

The escrow company is normally chosen by the buyer or seller, but is often directed by either agent involved in the transaction, as they may already have a working relationship with an escrow company. Be aware that it is ultimately your choice in selecting your escrow company, based on your needs and wants.

How Can We Prepare for Escrow?

Communication is the key to limiting the stress and pressure of obtaining loan approval, processing escrow and planning a move. Common closing delays are caused in the following areas:

- If any of the buyers or sellers will be out of town prior to the escrow closing date, contact your loan processor and escrow officer to discuss scheduling.
- Do not incur additional debt or change your employment status. Your credit and employment may be verified again as late as the escrow closing date.
- Make sure you have a valid picture ID required for closing document notarization (current driver's license, passport).
- Apply for homeowner insurance coverage right away. Don't wait to the last minute, as coverage availability may be limited.
- All closing funds must clear the escrow trust account before escrow closing (wire transfers usually clear within two to six hours of origination; California cashier's checks usually clear 24 to 48 hours after deposit; official, corporate or personal checks may take longer and cause closing delays).

What Are Closing Costs?

Closing costs differ depending on the type of transaction involved. Escrow fees are based on the value of the escrow, for example, sales price and refinance loan amount, but these may vary based on the complexity or additional services required. Other fees that may be incurred during the escrow are new loan financing charges, title fees, commissions, payoff to existing lender and notary services. The escrow holder has no control over the fees that are charged by outside parties. It is your right to request a closing statement to review prior to the close of escrow.

Why Is a "Refundable Pad" Listed on My Estimated Closing Statement?

Although the escrow holder completes an estimate prior to closing escrow, items such as fees and interest may change daily. A refundable pad is used to avoid any shortages when closing escrow. Any unused portion of the pad will be refunded at the close of the transaction.

Can Escrow Accept a Personal Check at the Time of Closing?

The escrow holder must have a cashier's check drawn on a California bank or funds wired in order to close escrow in a timely manner. This is because escrow funds must be "good" or cleared prior to the close of escrow. Personal checks can be accepted; however, it will take up to 10 days to verify funds and for the check to clear.

At Closing, When Can the Seller Expect to Receive the Net Proceeds?

Once documents have been recorded, the escrow holder must wait for the wire transfer from the title company. This is usually received the day after recording. Upon receipt of said funds, the escrow holder must balance the file and can then issue checks and closing statements.

Source: Allison-McCloskey Escrow Company, California **http://www.allisonmccloskeyescrow.com**.

What You Need to Know about Title Insurance

Title insurance in the United States is indemnity insurance against financial loss from defects in title to real property, and from the invalidity or unenforceability of mortgage liens. Title insurance is principally a product developed and sold in the US as a result of the comparative deficiency of the US land records laws. It is meant to protect an owner's or a lender's financial interest in real property against loss due to title defects, liens or other matters. It will defend against a lawsuit attacking the title as it is insured, or reimburse the insured for the actual monetary loss incurred, up to the dollar amount of insurance provided by the policy. The first title insurance company, the Law Property Assurance and Trust Society, was formed in Pennsylvania in 1853. The vast majority of title insurance policies are written on land within the US.

Typically, the real property interests insured are fee simple ownership or a mortgage. However, title insurance can be purchased to insure any interest in real property, including an easement, lease or life estate. Just as lenders require fire insurance and other types of insurance coverage to protect their investment, nearly all-institutional lenders also require title insurance to protect their interest in the collateral of loans secured by real estate. Some mortgage lenders, especially non-institutional lenders, may not require title insurance.

Title insurance is available in many other countries, such as Canada, Australia, United Kingdom, Northern Ireland, Mexico, New Zealand, China, Korea and throughout Europe. However, while a substantial number of properties located in these countries are insured by US title insurers, they do not constitute a significant share of the real estate transactions in those countries. They also do not constitute a large share of US title insurers' revenues. In many cases, these are properties to be used for commercial purposes by US companies doing business abroad, or properties financed by US lenders. The US companies involved buy title insurance to obtain the security of a US insurer backing up the evidence of title that they receive from the other country's land registration system, and payment of legal defense costs if the title is challenged.

Source: **www.wikipedia.org**.

The Top 3 Considerations When Making Large Cross-Border Purchases

1. Lock-in Cost
- Where two currencies are involved, you will be exposed to foreign currency exchange fluctuations. As you get more serious about a property, begin reviewing where the US dollar is, relative to the Canadian dollar, to understand the currency premium or discount you will be paying on top of the purchase price.
- Once you understand the relative cost/savings the currency exchange represents, ensure you consider locking in that cost. Through the utilization of a series of currency exchange products available on the market today, you can secure today's rates

for next month's purchase, so you won't have any surprises when it comes time to close.

2. Work Out Logistics

- Working with foreign real estate agents and lawyers is typically the easier way to manage the money transfer and property closing process when making a cross-border purchase. You must ensure that the foreign currency transaction is completed in a timely manner, so the logistics of exchanging funds does not interfere with getting the final payment to the appropriate party before the close of sale.

- Working with an international payments company can help take the stress out of this process. Reputable firms will ensure the foreign exchange transaction is executed in a timely manner and, in addition, will instruct the delivery of the domestic funds to the seller's account in time for the close.

3. After-Purchase Considerations

- So, you've bought a property in a foreign country, now what? Consider that you may have either expected or unexpected expenses related to that property on a regular basis. These could include anything from regular mortgage payments to maintenance or repair costs as the property ages. How will you manage these payments on a regular basis, while minimizing your currency fluctuation risk?

- You have options for setting up recurring payments or for sending lump-sum payments across the border. Your options will also vary depending on if you have a bank account in the domestic currency of the property and if you don't hold a local account. A good course of action is to work with an international payments company to develop a payment lifeline to your property in the event of the unexpected while minimizing your expenses on the reoccurring, expected, payments.

Source: Custom House.

7 Mistakes People Make When Hiring a Property Manager

Often investors don't realize that the due diligence required in hiring a good property management company is just as important as the due diligence required when purchasing the property. In fact, the value of the investment is dependent upon it.

1. Checking References—Finding the right property manager can make the difference between a good investment and a poor one. It is important to get referrals from present clients of the property management company you are considering. You must follow through and make the calls as you need to get an idea if the quality of service the company is promising will continue once the contract has been signed.

2. Property Management Agreement—It is important before signing any management agreement to fully understand all costs and obligations involved for the property owner. Most property management contracts are lengthy and often use language that a new investor may not be familiar with. The costs involved are usually not verbally explained, unless you ask. Read the contract from beginning to end, and when in doubt, ask for clarification. The normal costs involved with hiring a property manager include a one-time set-up fee (normally around $100 per property), a leasing fee (6% of the yearly lease amount, one time) and a management fee (10% of the rental income, paid monthly). The leasing fee is taken out of the first month's rent and is charged to cover the advertising costs and time spent finding and placing a tenant. Some companies will charge an advertising fee instead of the leasing fee, but be sure that you are not being charged for both.

3. Long-Term Tenant Lease—The most important thing to remember with regard to the management contract is to ensure that that the manager does not allow a tenant to sign a lease for longer than one year. It might initially appear that having a tenant sign a two- or three-year lease would be an ideal situation. However, when you sign the initial contract, you have to agree to pay the management fees for the duration of the lease. If you decide to leave the company for any reason, they will keep all remaining months of management fees. This is for the full duration of the lease and the funds will be deducted from your management account.

4. Manager's Location—I cannot stress enough how big this one is and how often it's overlooked. It is extremely important to ensure that the person responsible for the rental and sight inspections of your property lives and works on the same side of the city that the property is located. This makes a huge difference in the amount of attention your property will receive. This is especially true for the times when it is vacant and numerous trips have to be made to and from the location. Property managers are human and they often neglect properties that are too far out of their way. Many will take them on even if they know they will not be able to manage them properly.

5. Trusting that Your Property is a Priority—Even when you have a good manager, don't presume that he/she is on top of all the enquiries that come in for your vacant units. They deal with so many calls and emails in a day that many interested parties never get their enquiries acknowledged quickly or at all. If your property is not rented out in a timely manner, help your manager find a tenant. I'm not talking about getting overly involved with the process, because that can lead to a lot of confusion and frustration. Simply run a free ad on an Internet advertising site, such as Craigslist, including a description and photograph of your property. It's a good idea to repost the ad every three days for good exposure. Respond to all enquiries quickly and give them your property manager's name and phone number. Email your manager advising them to expect a call and request a follow-up for the next day to see how things are progressing. I would even go as far as emailing the interested prospect back to see if they were responded to in a timely manner.

6. Going with the Cheapest—Do not hire the most inexpensive company you can find. Some companies charge only 8% for the management fee but often lack in service. The money you save on the fee could be lost from poor management.

7. Contractor Pricing—Get your own quote occasionally when you need plumbers, flooring companies or repairmen to service your property. This will ensure you're getting a competitive price. As well, read your monthly statement carefully for any excessive or incorrect charges.

It may be necessary to manage your managers every now and again, but it's worth the time spent. It's still a lot easier and less work than managing the property yourself. Once you have found a great manager and know for sure that things are running efficiently, take a breather and be thankful that you're not unclogging the toilet.

Source: Wendy L. Fedoruk, president of US Property 101.

TED'S TIPS

- Hire a title/escrow company to close your property purchase and help you get title insurance.

- Some realtors will want the vendor and purchaser to have the same escrow company and for a deposit to be placed with that escrow company.

- On the day of closing, water, gas and electric meters will be read and the seller will be responsible for the utility usage up until that day. You may also need to make deposits with both the water and electric companies.

- If you plan to take over any service contracts from the seller, you will owe him or her the unused portion of those contracts that have been pre-paid, such as security system fees, pest control, pool and/or lawn services or home maintenance contracts.

- Expect to have to process LOTS of paper.

- Some banks now require a full T-1 tax return for mortgage applications.

- Hooking up utilities as a non-resident sometimes requires a larger deposit.

Currency

Currency and Emotions

In 2007 when the Canadian dollar hit parity with the US, I was in my local gym and a loud shout went up that was followed by clapping which startled me at first. I looked up to see the recent parity announcement on the television but assumed that I had just missed a sports newsflash about the local hockey team. I turned to one of the patrons and asked what all the fuss was about. She told me with some excitement about the currency situation but described it like Canada had just beaten the US in a hockey game.

While the performance of the Canadian dollar versus the US is important to trade and investment, I can't help

---

but think that something a little deeper lies in the Canadian relationship with the US dollar. The relationship in Canada with the US dollar is unusual from an international point of view and like nothing I have witnessed before. Given the fact that many Canadians feel that they sit in the shadow of the US, it makes sense that in some way Canadians allow currency to define who they are internationally.

Currency and Real Estate

While currency risk is a very important factor when considering a foreign investment, I personally feel there is way too much emphasis on the strength of the dollar in recent years as a key motivator to the timing of a real estate purchase. So what do I mean by this?

I believe one must focus on the deal and not allow currency to make the decision for them. Many Canadians traveled south when the dollar got close to parity and felt they got a bargain as a result, since house prices were off and they did well with the currency exchange. Sounds logical.

Some of the people who bought at that time have had further real estate price declines, and any savings they made on the currency has been wiped out. You see, if you focus first and foremost on the real estate deal and whether it fits for you, currency should be a factor but not the main feature.

Also, why focus on saving 10-15% on currency when prices are down in some areas 50%? Just because the Canadian dollar is on par or close to par does not make it a time to buy real estate in the United States.

If the property fits your plan and the deal makes sense, then the deal makes sense, in the same way that real estate appreciation should be the bonus while the cashflow is the focus if your timing is correct. And if the dollar is good to you, then great.

Currency and the Future

In short, no one knows what the dollar will do in the future, but that does not mean there are no speculators out there. Many expect to see parity again sooner than it was last achieved, and some are even speculating that some day Canadians will be getting two or even three US dollars for one Canadian if the US dollar is dramatically devalued.

Source: Philip McKernan Inc., **www.philipmckernan.com**.

11

Victory

Ted was still booting up the computer on his first day back in the office after his trip to Phoenix when his boss rang him.

"Can you meet me in my office, please?" Jack asked.

"Um, sure," Ted said. He then hung up the phone. Jack wasn't known for being upbeat, but the tone of his voice was serious. Ted had a queasy feeling in his stomach.

"They can't fire me for taking so much vacation time, can they?" he thought to himself.

While it's true he had been away a lot in the past six to eight months looking for property, he wasn't overbooked on his vacation days. Was he? Ted felt nervous. He stood up from his chair and straightened his tie.

"Calm down, Ted," he said to himself. "The boss just wants to talk. Business isn't so bad. My performance has been good. I've received a bonus every year since I started."

Ted walked down the hall towards Jack's office. He knocked on the door.

"You wanted to see me, Jack?" Ted said, pretending to be calm.

"Yes, Ted. Have a seat," said Jack, a slightly overweight man in his early 60s. He was wearing a pinstriped shirt, suspenders and a red tie with a couple of visible coffee stains.

"So, Ted. You've been away a lot in the past few months, haven't you?" Jack leaned forward in his chair and crossed his hands on the desk in front of him.

"Um, yeah . . . is there a problem?" Ted asked.

"Problem?" Jack said. "Well, I don't think so. I mean, you tell me. How did those trips work out for you? I overheard some guys in the lunchroom saying you were buying an investment property down south. They said you bought a townhouse in Phoenix. Got yourself a good deal, too."

Ted took a deep breath and then exhaled quickly.

"Yeah, that's right," he said, still worried about the purpose behind him being called to the boss's office.

"Well, Ted, you see . . ." Jack began, then sat back in his chair and folded his arms across the top of his stomach. "My wife wants us to start thinking about retirement. She thinks we should buy something in the US. She's been watching a lot of TV, reading the business pages. Says there are some good deals down there."

Ted's face suddenly relaxed. Jack continued talking.

"I was thinking, well, if a guy like you can do it, well so can I," said Jack.

Ted laughed to himself. He let Jack keep talking.

"So, I was wondering, Ted, can you tell me a little bit more about how you did it?" Jack said, looking at Ted as though he was about to share some sort of secret information.

Ted paused for a moment and stared back at his boss, who, for the first time he could remember, was actually asking him for advice, instead of giving it.

"Well, Jack. You're right, if a guy like me can do it, I guess anyone can," Ted said, although he knew the remark went over his boss's head.

"Oh, Ted, I didn't mean it like that," Jack interrupted. "Don't get all sensitive on me. But you know what I mean. You aren't exactly Mr. Dealmaker."

Ted had to admit that might be true. However, his experience looking for property over the past several months taught him a lot about business—and life. It taught him a lot about himself, in fact. He could do anything he put his mind to. All he needed was a little direction—and a plan.

All of a sudden, Ted had a vision of standing up, leaning over his boss's desk, sweeping it clear of the piles of paper and a hot coffee, and yelling "I quit!"

"Ted, are you okay?" Jack said, waking Ted from his fantasy.

Ted smiled.

"Tell you what, Jack," Ted said. "How about we meet for lunch this week and talk about it? I can tell you all about how I did it. It was a lot of hard work. We can also discuss that raise I have been asking about for the past year or more, the one you promised was coming to me?"

Jack rocked back and forth in his chair. He smiled back at Ted.

"Sounds like a good plan, Ted," said Jack. "How about Thursday, then?"

"I'll check my schedule and get back to you," Ted said. He then stood up, shook Jack's hand and turned to walk out of the office.

"Nice to have you back at work, Ted," Jack said. "A guy like you is missed when you're not around."

As Ted put his hand on the doorknob to leave, he turned to Jack. "Can I ask you, what do you want from a property in the States?"

Jack, who had already begun to dial the phone, stopped and put down the receiver.

"What do you mean?"

"Do you want to use it for private use, as a retirement place for part of the year, or do you want to rent it out part or all year round?"

Jack looked a little uncomfortable. He responded defensively: "An investment, Ted. Yeah, that's right, an investment."

Ted, who couldn't believe that he was confronting his boss, continued: "So you're looking for cash flow, or are you buying hoping the market goes up so you can make money?"

Jack, who had his arms crossed, said, "Well, my wife wants to spend the winters down there in the next few years and I'm not sure if that's for me."

"Well," Ted said, "before we have lunch on Thursday, you and your wife need to sit down and get clear on what you want this property to do for you and get really clear on why you are buying in the US. There are many options available, and if you're not clear what you want, it's going to be very challenging to advise you."

"So, Ted, where do you start with something like this?" Jack asked.

Ted walked over to the large white board in Jack's office and picked up the eraser beside it. He then looked at Jack. "Do you mind?" Ted asked, looking at the sales targets on the board.

"No, no, go ahead," Jack replied, obviously intrigued. Ted picked up a black marker and starting drawing what looked like a sales graph starting at the bottom left and gradually drew a line to the top right of the board.

"I like the look of these figures. Is this the money I will make in the US, Ted?" Jack asked.

Ted, who was focused on the drawing, stopped at the top of the board and then drew a line downward to the bottom of the right-hand side.

"Oh, this doesn't look too good," Jack said.

"Now, Jack, let's pretend this is a mountain and this is you on the left at the bottom," Ted said as he drew a little circle with arms and legs.

"Now, let's say this mountain represents a goal you want to achieve like a buying a property, or any other goal for that matter," Ted said.

Jack liked this new authoritative side to Ted that he hadn't seen before.

"So, Jack, you want to climb to the summit, which is the final goal. What is the first thing you would do?"

"Well, I guess I would take the first step, Ted," Jack said.

"And then what would you do?" Ted asked.

"Take the next step, and the next and so on till I hit the top," Jack said.

"No," Ted replied. It's the first time he had used that word with his boss. "Before you take one single step, you would need to be prepared for the climb, have the right team and have a plan for the route you're going to take."

Jack smiled. "That makes total sense, Ted. So, what you're saying is I need to have a plan before I look to buy anything?"

"Yes, Jack. It's the single biggest thing I learned in the process. Think about it like you are at base camp and about to start the climb."

Jack appeared completely engaged. "So, once I get a plan in place and find the right team, I am ready to go to the top?"

"Well, you have to acclimatize along the way," Ted said.

"What?" Jack said, interrupting.

"Never mind, we will cover that later. For now, let's just focus on the plan," Ted said.

"So, Ted, where did you get all this from?" Jack asked.

"My buddy, Sid. He is kind of a mentor to me."

"He's like your own personal Sherpa for the climb, Ted!" Jack said, laughing.

"Well, I guess you're right Jack, he is."

Ted put the marker down, looked at Jack and said, "Don't try to climb Everest without trying other smaller mountains. It's all about patience. In society today, we want everything now. We want to get to the top of our own Everest, but we want to take the cable car and don't want to do all the climbing," Ted preached.

"Wow, Ted, I should have you speak to the sales team about this stuff. And maybe it's a good idea to bring Donna along with me.

"I would be honored to talk to you both," Ted said and then headed for the door.

Just then, Jack shouted, "Perhaps, Ted, you can be our Sherpa and guide us through this US real estate stuff?"

Ted turned and looked at Jack. "I will tell you everything I know, but I'm not going to carry your bags for you!"

He smiled, then walked out and closed the door behind him.

Outside the office door, Ted paused for a moment. He felt proud of himself at work for the first time in a long time.

REMATCH

Ted and Sid were concentrating hard on the board game in front of them. This time it was Ted who had the smug grin. Sid looked more concerned.

"I cannot believe you managed to get control of so much of the world, Ted," Sid said. "I must still be suffering from jet lag. Maybe it's the Vancouver low-pressure area. Or did you put something in my drink?"

Ted laughed. Sid was starting to panic at the prospect of losing the game to Ted.

"Don't use that jet lag excuse on me," Ted said. "I'm beating you fair and square. I have a plan—and it's working."

Sid only had two territories left on the board in front of him. "You know, Ted, you wouldn't be winning if I hadn't taught you everything I know," Sid said.

Sid threw the dice. With a shout of glee, Ted leaned over and took Sid's red army piece and moved into the last territory Sid's army held.

Ted could taste victory.

Sid tried to distract him. "So, Ted, are you really going to buy another property later this year? If so, where?"

Ted didn't take his eye off the game. "Don't try and distract me, Sid. Watch this space and all will be revealed."

Ted, who had amassed his large army on the border, looking ominously over at Sid's one little red army piece, couldn't help but smirk.

"You're loving this, aren't you?" Sid asked.

"I have waited a long time for this day," Ted said. "Now, roll the dice!"

Sid, who has resigned himself to defeat, threw the dice. He had officially lost the game.

Ted calmly leaned forward. He took the dice in one hand, gave them a kiss and smiled.

"See, Sid, I can be a winner just like you. All I needed was a little confidence."

Epilogue

For many Canadians with a little extra cash, the idea of buying property in the US seems like a no-brainer. The weather is warmer, especially in the southern states, the language is the same and the cultural differences are not that dramatic. Many Canadians have been working hard and saving for years to buy a home away from home, in particular to get a break from those harsh winters. Others have come into money either through an inheritance or increasing equity in their own home over the years. And when the Canadian dollar is high, compared to its US counterpart, the urge to buy increases even more. The result: The American dream, for many, has become the Canadian dream.

There is no doubt in my mind that there are investment opportunities in the US, especially now that prices are down considerably from the peak in 2006, and the selection is wide. That said, cheap and plentiful housing are not the only reasons to take the US real estate plunge. What concerns me is that not enough people are sitting down and really asking themselves WHY they are buying.

As well, too many are neglecting to consider exactly WHAT they should buy. Many investors' first thought is to grab a lifestyle property—something they can live in when they are old and gray. What they don't consider is their own lifestyle and if they will really use that property as often as they think. There is also the so-called "hybrid" option, where buyers can use the property for part of the year and rent it out for the rest. The last option, of course, is buying an investment property and renting it out, hopefully building equity. The last two options are great for cash flow, but also require a lot of work, as has been explained throughout South of 49.

What I can't stress enough is realizing the difference between the type of property purchases, and deciding which option is best for you. Then, once you've made that decision, there is another important thing to check before buying—your emotions. In my experience, every investor gets emotional at deal time. Buying property is one of the biggest investments people make in their lives, and getting emotional when spending such huge sums of money is human. However, the difference between a smart investor and one with buyer's remorse is that the wise ones know how to manage their emotions.

I have personally invested in real estate in more than six different countries and have to admit that ego played a huge part at the beginning. I thought it would be cool to talk about the different properties I owned in locations around the world. I thought people would be impressed by what I had achieved. But my ego—the need to impress others—ran counter to making sound business decisions.

A great example of how we are driven by emotion is hidden in a simple supply-and-demand business story. After hundreds of thousands of British tourists descended on Spain's beachfront resorts, they acquired a taste for a local beer. A UK tourist and businessman decided he would try to make a profit by importing this local Spanish beer to the UK, and sell it there. This businessman purchased thousands of cases of the brew and put it up for sale in the UK. For the first few weeks, the beer flew off the shelves. But then, almost overnight, sales died. After researching the reason for the drop in sales, he discovered that people felt the beer was somehow different from what they drank while visiting Spain. It wasn't. In fact, what he learned is that people were not buying the beer, but the experience. They were buying the emotion of being on holiday in Spain, sitting under the hot sun next to the water. That same emotion attached to this taste was absent at home in the UK.

How does this relate to real estate, you ask? Consider how many people have purchased property after being on vacation, after getting a taste of the so-called "good life," only to later regret it. Too often, investors get caught up in the emotion of owning property, inspired by this dream.

Being Irish, born and raised in Dublin, I know a lot about how over-exuberance can get the better of a once-practical population. Starting in the mid 1990s, in a period of rapid economic growth known as the Celtic Tiger, Ireland was transformed from one of the poorest countries in Western Europe to one of the wealthiest. The surge in prosperity led to a rise in property values, which meant Irish homeowners suddenly became wealthy on paper. The Celtic Tiger also brought with it a sense of confidence, where the idea of investing outside the borders of their own country was no longer intimidating.

With their newfound "wealth," and given the rising prices of property at home in Ireland, many looked beyond the border to fulfill their dream of further capitalizing on increasing real estate values. Many looked to Eastern Europe, where housing was still cheap, believing real estate there just had to go up at the same pace as in the more wealthy European nations. That didn't happen. The market fundamentals were weak and many of the investments led to significant financial loss.

Watching this happen to investors in Ireland and the UK, and knowing first-hand the consequences of not investing wisely with a prudent plan in hand, was the inspiration for this book. Many Canadians are being lured south to the United States to buy real estate because it appears cheap. As far as I'm concerned, a good deal is only good if the fundamentals are strong.

While this book ends with Ted eventually buying a place, it doesn't mean you should, too. Don't do what Ted does, if it doesn't fit your plan. Instead, use this book as a guide that challenges your motivation behind a possible purchase. If you're sure you want to buy a property in the US, do it with your eyes open.

In the end, Ted made the "smart" choice, but many people make a choice that they later regret. I felt that a deeper understanding of the pros and cons of a lifestyle versus an investment purchase would be of benefit to you, the reader. With that in mind, we have presented an alternate scenario of what would have happened to Ted had he ignored Sid's sage advice. This alternate ending is available as a download at **www.southof49.com.** In addition, you will find additional resources and information on upcoming South of 49 seminars about buying in the United States.

"Success is manufactured in the mind, while happiness is cultivated in the soul."

—*Philip McKernan*

WANT MORE?

SOUTH OF 49 —SECOND ENDING

What if Ted took a different path?

Download the second ending to *SOUTH OF 49* for **FREE** to discover the outcome when Ted ignores Sid's advice and allows emotion to get in the way of his decision. Visit www. southof49.com to download.

SOUTH OF 49 —WORKSHOPS

To register for upcoming workshops on how to invest in the US Real Estate Market, go to www.southof49.com.

SOUTH OF 49 —SPEAKER

Are you looking to hire a Speaker for a Real Estate or Investment event? Visit www.southof49.com for more information.

SOUTH OF 49 —RESOURCES

Download critical estate forms and tools at www.south49.com.

www.southof49.com

PHILIP MCKERNAN

International Speaker & Trainer

Are you looking for a Speaker to truly engage and inspire your audience?

Philip's passion and good Irish wit may be exactly what you are looking for.

What you will get?

You are guaranteed to get a Speaker who is PASSIONATE about life, REAL about what it takes to make change, and BOLD in his questioning and storytelling.

What Topics?

- SOUTH OF 49
- THE POWER OF CONFIDENCE
- THE PURSUIT OF WEALTH & HAPPINESS

What Industry or Events?

Philip speaks internationally to Real Estate and Business groups. Ideal for Sales Incentive Events, Conferences, Annual Retreats, Team Building, or Client Appreciation Events.

www.philipmckernan.com

Index

A

accountant
  and cost segregation, 118
  and cross-border issues, 119
  and LOC, 89
  and tax advice, 91
  and US taxes, 112
accrued gains, and trust, 100
adjustable rate mortgage,
  California, 130
after-purchase considerations,
  227–228
agreement, property
  management, 229
agriculture, Florida, 67
AIG, 87
all-cash buyers, California, 129
Alligator mississippiensis, 68
aluminum wiring, 208
annual exemptions, US estate
  tax, 98
appraisals
  LOC, 90
  and mortgage, 202
  and short sale, 130
Arizona facts, 164–165
"as is" property, California, 129
athlete, 106
attic ventilation, 208
attribution rules, income tax, 99
auction
  bidding, 146–147
  California, 128, 129
  check list, 144
  Q&A, 148–149

  steps, listed, 151–155
automated teller bank machine,
  68
average income, neighborhood,
  84

B

Baby Boomers, 51, 85
bank-owned properties
  California, 128
  chart, 127
  and mortgage, 153
  unsold at auction, 128
banks
  Canadian, 90–91
  US, 88
the Benwood, 68
Biscayne National Park, 67
breathing exercise, 214
"buy and hold," 187

C

Canada-US Income Tax
  Convention, 107
Canada-US Tax Treaty, 98, 107,
  109, 114
Canadian banks in US, 90–91
Canadian income tax,
  attribution rules, 99
Canadian tax, US property
  on capital gain, 111–112
  and foreign tax credit,
    114–115
  strategies, 117–118
capital gains

exemption, 115
and family trust, 100
US and Canada, 111, 112
cash
flow, and HELOC, 90
types for investing, 188–190
cash flow comparable tool, 172
Celtic Tiger, 245–246
certified public accountant, US, 119
charitable sports event, 106
chartered accountant, Canada, 119
chasing the market, 83
Clearwater, 68
closer-connection exception, 104–106
closing
costs, 223–224
in escrow, 221
settlement, 220–221
CMHC, 87
Coachella Valley, 138–139
condominium, 40
construction, Florida, 67
contacts, defined, 105–106
contractor pricing, 231
copper wiring, 208
costs
LOC, 90
property management, 231
cost segregation analysis, 118
Craigslist, 230
credit
approval, mortgage, 202
crisis, US, 88
and equity, 90
markets, US, 202

currency, 232–234
currency exchange products, 226–227
current market value, and equity, 87

D
deductions
for business and investments, 119
for depreciation, 118
and late filing, 111
rental income, 110
deposit, auction, 154
depreciation, 110, 118
developments, neighborhood, 84
disclosure requirements, California, 131
Disney, 42
"Disney Dream Experience," 49
Disney Vacation Club, 48–49
driver's license, and financing, 201

E
earth-wood contact, 209
easements, 225
Economic Development Office, 84
economic relations, and residency, 107
economy
Florida, 66–67
and property market, 83
emotion
and currency, 232–233
and real estate, 83–84, 244–245

employers, neighborhood, 84
entities (taxpayers), 118
equity
    accessing, 87–88
    appreciation, 182–183
    calculating, 90
    and foreclosure, 129
Equity Take Out (ETO), 88, 90
escrow, 221, 222–224
estate planning, 69, 98–101
estate tax, US, 98–100
estimated closing statement, 224
Evergaldes National Park, 67
exempt individual exception,
    106–107
exemption
    estate tax, 98
    and principal residence, 115
    withholding tax, 110–111
Exemption from Withholding
    Tax (Form 4224), 111

F
Fakahatchee Strand, 68
family trust, 99–100
fees
    and auction, 155
    escrow, 223
    and first bid, 152
    and foreclosure, 129, 130
    legal, 90
    realtor, 86
fee simple ownership, 225
filing requirements, US income
    tax, 111, 114
financial planner, 91
financing
    and Canadian banks in US,
    90–91

closing, and cost, 223
and foreclosures, 130
for foreign nationals, 201–
    202
rules for, 88–91
flooding, 208
Florida info
    economy, 66–67
    facts, 66
    trivia, 67–69
    weather, seasons, 65
foreclosure, California, 127–131,
    151–153
foreign currency exchange, 226,
    227–228
foreign estate agents, lawyers,
    227
foreign government related
    individual, 106
Foreign Investment in Real
    Property Tax Act, 113–114
foreign tax credit, 114, 118
Form 4224, 110
Form 1040 NR, 111
Fort Lauderdale (Venice of
    America), 69
foundation problems, 208
Freedom 55, 74
furnaces, 209
future, and currency, 233–234
F visa, 106

G
galvanized steel pipes, 209
Gatorade, 68
gentrification, neighborhood, 85
Genworth Financial, 87
Green, Benjamin, 68
gross rental income, 109

"growth atmosphere,"
neighborhood, 84

H

habitual abode, and residency,
107
health technology, Florida, 67
high-ratio mortgage, and equity,
87–88
Hilton, 42
home equity, 87–88
Home Equity Line of Credit
(HELOC), 88–91
home inspection, 204–209
Hyatt, 42
hybrid property, 178

I

Immigration and Naturalization
Service, 108
Individual Taxpayer
Identification Number, 112,
117
insurance
homeowner, and escrow, 223
life, 100
premium, mortgage, 88
as rental income deductible,
110
title, 131, 225, 226
interest
LOC, 90
new mortgage, 89
rates, US, 88
interest-only payments
(IIELOC), 89
Internal Revenue Code, 110
international payment
companies, 227, 228

international trade, Florida, 66
Interval International (II), 42
investing
in rental property, 187–188
strategies, cash, 188–190
vs speculating, 83–85
investment property, 178, 191,
202
investment rich, cash poor, 189
IRS forms, listed, 119–120
Islamorada, 69

J

job creation, neighborhood, 84
joint tenancy, 99
J visa, 106

K

Kennedy Space Center, 66
Key West, 68

L

"landlording," 187
Las Vegas, 141–142
Law Property Assurance and
Trust Society, 225
lawyer, 92
lead paint, 208
leases, 225
legal fees, LOC, 90
"leverage income," 189
liens
and auction, 152, 153
clearing, California, 128, 129,
131
and title insurance, 225
life estates, 225
life insurance, and US estate tax
bill, 100

lifestyle property, 178
lifestyle scorecard, 178–180
lightning strikes, Clearwater, 68
limited liability companies, 118
Line of Credit (LOC), 89–91
liquid reserves, 201, 202
location, property management, 230
lock-in cost, 226
long-term values, 84–85
lump-sum payments, 227–228

M
maintenance, as deductible, 110
Marriott, 42
moonstone, 68
mortgage
  broker, 91
  and equity, 87
  insurance, 87–88
  interest, 110
  life insurance, 88
M visa, 106

N
negotiation tips, 213–215
net rental income, and US tax, 110
non-resident alien, 103, 104, 109
non-resident withholding tax, 110
notice of default, California, 128, 129
notice of trustee sale, California, 128

O
overbidding, auction, 154
ownership

personal, 98–99
personal, in joint tenancy, 99
through Canadian corporation, 100
through Canadian partnership, 100
through Canadian trust, 99–100
and transfer of property, 101
and US estate tax, 98–101

P
"passive income," 188
passive loss rules, 118
passport, to get financing, 201
permanent home, and residency, 107
permanent residence visa, US, 107–108
permanent resident status, US, 106
personal debt service, and HELOC, 90
personal ownership
  and joint tenancy, 99
  and US estate tax, 98–99
personal relations, and residency, 107
Phoenix, 23–24
Phoenix facts, 163–164
population, neighborhood, 84
pre-foreclosure, California, 128
principal, new mortgage, 89
principal residence
  exemption, 115
  and HELOC, 89
problems, neighborhood, 85
properly values, 83–85
property management

advantages, 185–187
choosing, 186–187
as fundamental, 85
hiring, 228–231
as research tool, 170–171
and withholding tax, 109,
110
property market, and economy,
83
property taxes, 110

R
real estate, and currency, 233–
234
real estate agent, 85–87, 92
RealtyChase, 152
recreation property
as lifestyle property, 178
and Snowbirds, 109
as vacation property, 201
recurring payments, 227–228
references, property
management, 228
refinancing
mortgage, 88–89
and notice of default, 128
"refundable pad," 224
renewal, neighborhood, 85
rental income
and flat tax, 110
and management fee, 229
tax implications, 109
rental properties, 170–171
renting, and US tax, 109–112
REO (Real Estate Owned),
California, 128, 130–131
residency permit, US, 108
resident alien
and rental property, 109

and substantial presence test,
103
and tax return, 111
vs non-resident, 104
Resort Condominiums
International (RCI), 42
resort condominium units, 41
"retirement" lifestyle, 190
"right to use" (timeshares), 41
risk
and currency fluctuation, 227,
233
and goals, 187
and investment, 41
reducing, 84
rollerbladers, and ATM, 68
roof repairs, 208

S
Saint Augustine, 67
Saint John's River, 68
sandbox rules, financing, 88
Santa Ana, 135–136
second mortgage (LOC), 89
selling US property, 113–115
service industry, Florida, 67
settlement (closing), 220–221
shared property, 69
shipwreck, 68
short sale, California, 128
short-sale property, California,
129–130
"Snowbirds," 109
social security number, 117
software industry, Florida, 67
space industry, Florida, 66–67
speculating vs investing, 83–85
spousal trust, 99
Starwood, 42

state foreclosure laws, auction, 152
student, 106
substantial presence test, 102–108
suntan cream, 68
swamps, 68–69

T
taking ownership, auction, 154–155
tax
  credit, 114, 115
  home, 105, 106
  laws, 107–108
  property, 110
  return, US, 108
  returns, US, 110
  strategies, US properties, 117–119
tax-deductible interest, HELOC, 89
tenants, evicting, California, 128, 129, 131
tenants-in-common, 99
1031/like-kind exchange rules, 118
termites, 209
timeshare, 40, 41–42, 48–49
the time trap, 214
time zones, 69
title company, and closing, 221
title insurance
  California, 131
  explained, 225–226
top ten questions (why buy), 40–41
tourism, Florida, 66
town home, 40

transfer disclosure statement, California, 131
transfer of US real estate, 101
transportation, neighborhood, 85
travel, costs and time, 69
treaty tie-breaker exception, 107–108
21-year rule, 100

U
university research, Florida, 67
unsold property, California, 128
US
  citizens, and US estate tax, 98
  credit markets, 202
  estate tax, and family trust, 100
  land records laws, 225
  residency status, 102–104
  title insurers, 225–226
US Income Tax Regulations, 108
US Non-Resident Alien Income Tax Return, 111
utilities, 110

V
vacant units, property management, 230
vacation home
  defined, 201
  and liquid reserves, 201
"vacation ownership," 42
vacation property, 40
Venice of America (Fort Lauderdale), 69
ventilation, attic, 208

W

water pipes, 209
why buy (ten top questions),
  40–41
will, 69
withholding certificate, 114
withholding tax, 109–110, 113
Withlacoochee, 69
Wyndham, 42